John Ware Edgar

Report on a Visit to Sikhim and the Thibetan Frontier

In October, November, and December, 1873

John Ware Edgar

Report on a Visit to Sikhim and the Thibetan Frontier
In October, November, and December, 1873

ISBN/EAN: 9783337146757

Printed in Europe, USA, Canada, Australia, Japan

Cover: Foto ©ninafisch / pixelio.de

More available books at **www.hansebooks.com**

REPORT

ON

A VISIT TO SIKHIM AND THE THIBETAN FRONTIER

In October, November, and December, 1873.

By J. WARE EDGAR, Esq., C.S.I.,

Offg. Deputy Commissioner of Darjeeling.

Calcutta:
PRINTED AT THE BENGAL SECRETARIAT PRESS.
1874.

From J. WARE EDGAR, Esq.,
    Deputy Commissioner of Darjeeling,

To the COMMISSIONER of COOCH BEHAR.

    Darjeeling, the 20th January 1874.

Sir,

    As directed in Government order No. 3888 of the 8th October 1873, I have the honor to submit an account of my recent tour in Sikhim, together with such information as I have been able to collect on the state of affairs there; the condition, extent, and prospects of the trade with Thibet; the desirability of making a road or roads through Sikhim; the best route or routes to be taken; and the other points raised in the correspondence between the Government of Bengal and that of India.

    2. I take this opportunity of bringing to your notice and that of Government the great help I got during my whole trip from Lassoo Kazi, the Sikhim vakeel at Darjeeling; from Gellong, my Court interpreter; and from Tendook Mookhtear, the manager of the estate of the late Cheeboo Lama, who with his nephew accompanied me as volunteers without any out-look of profit. During the whole of my tour they worked untiringly at everything that came to their hands to do; and I am very anxious, with the permission of Government, to make them some acknowledgment for their good and voluntary service.

    I should like to give Tendook an inscribed silver Murwa Jug, and a Silver Watch to his nephew.

If this be allowed, I could pay for the things out of the unexpended balance of the sum of Rs. 2,000 sanctioned for presents to be made during the tour.

I have the honor to be,
Sir,
Your most obedient servant,

J. WARE EDGAR,
Deputy Commissioner.

PART I.

THE THIBETAN FRONTIER.

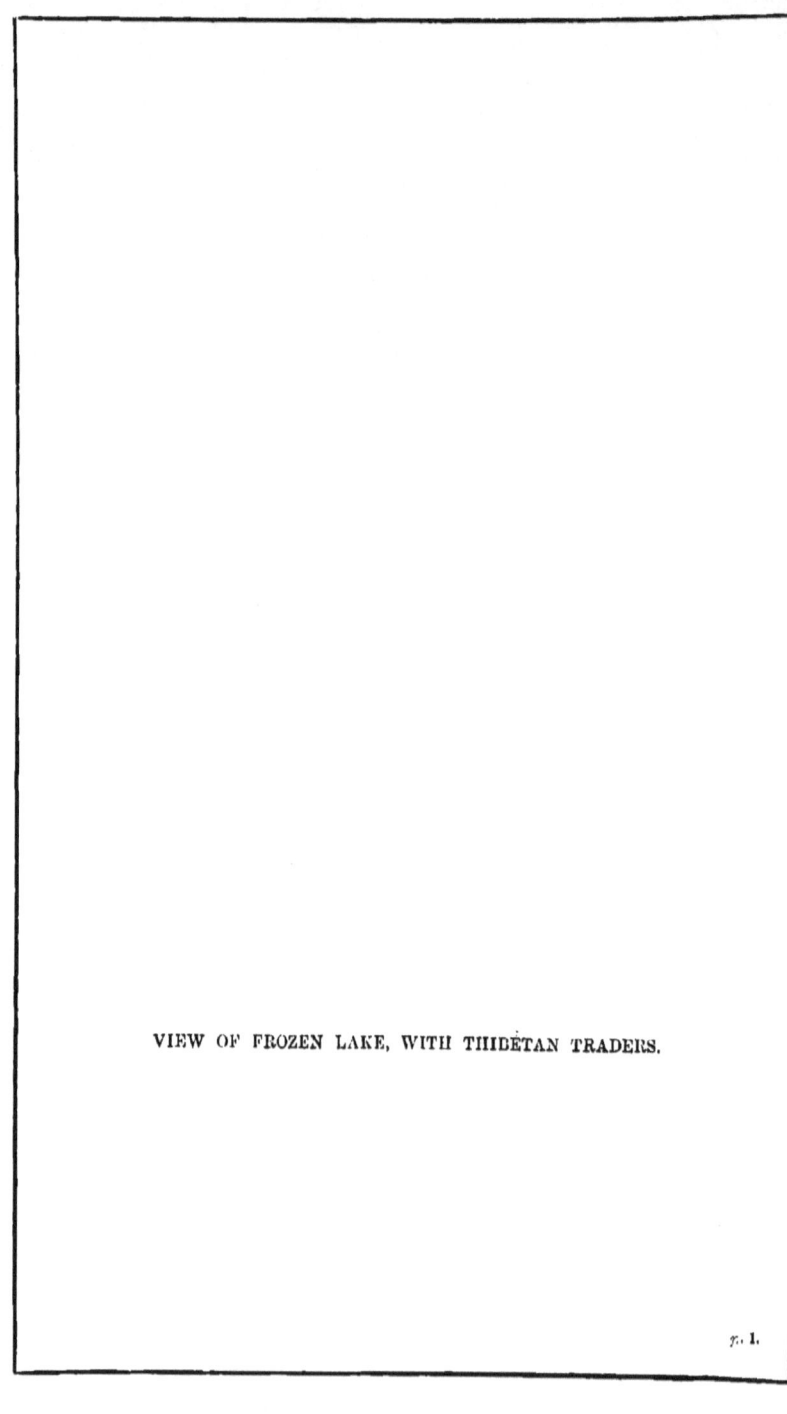

VIEW OF FROZEN LAKE, WITH THIBETAN TRADERS.

REPORT ON A VISIT TO SIKHIM AND THE THIBETAN FRONTIER.

Departure from Darjeeling.

I WAS fortunate enough at the outset to persuade Major Lindsay, R.E., to accompany me on at least a portion of the trip, and he undertook to make a rough survey of our routes as a help towards selecting a line of road if it should be ultimately decided that one was to be made. Unluckily some very necessary scientific instruments which I believe had been sent from Calcutta were not received by us, and our only means of taking heights were two aneroids, neither of which registered up to 12,000 feet.

Sikhim Frontier.

On the 23rd October we left Darjeeling, and on the following day reached Pheydoong, a village situated at an elevation of 4,892 feet on the south-east slope of the Dumsong spur, nearly forty miles from Darjeeling. Here we halted on the 25th, to make sure that all our preparations were complete, and on the morning of the 26th descended to the Rishi, which is here the boundary between our territory and Sikhim. The path is for a couple of miles very fair, running over wide natural terraces, some of which were cultivated and some fallow. After this there were some steep descents alternating with level ledges down to the river, which was crossed at a point about 2,800 feet below Pheydoong. The stream was narrow and fordable when we crossed it; but during the rains it becomes a formidable torrent eighty feet wide and ten or twelve feet deep.

Rheinock. The path on the other side of the river had been carefully zigzagged under the direction of an officer of the Sikhim State, who had been sent to put it in good order by the Rajah. It was rather steep in some places; but, on the whole, the ascent of 2,700 feet to the Rheinock slope, where we encamped, was not difficult. We greatly admired the rich cultivation and comfortable-looking homesteads scattered over the face of the Rheinock hill; but I afterwards saw much finer villages in the interior and longer-inhabited parts of Sikhim.

The Rilli. On the following day we crossed the Rheinock ridge at a point about six hundred feet higher than our camp, and then descended a not very difficult slope to a stream called the Rilli, which we crossed at about 2,817 feet. This stream is wider and deeper than the Rishi; but a bridge over it would probably cost less than one over the former stream. Before coming to the Rilli, we crossed a small stream called the Sa, which would also have to be crossed by a bridge during the rains. From the Rilli we ascended a very steep hill for 2,600 feet, to a confined place in the forest, much infested by *pipsas*, where we halted for the night.

The Lingtam. On the 28th we at first ascended some hundred feet to the Lingchung ridge, along which we went for some miles, at an elevation of upwards of 6,000 feet, through the heavy temperate forest, in which leeches most abound during the rains. We then descended a steep and bad path to a stream called the Lingtam, at about 4,800 feet. The Lingtam falls into the Rilli, and I think that a good road might be made with little difficulty along the bank of the latter stream to its junction with the

SIKHIM PEASANT'S HOUSE, WITH ORANGE TREES IN FRONT.

former, and then along the Lingtam to the point at which we crossed it, thus avoiding the troublesome ascent and descent of the Lingchung range. It is probable also that if this line were taken, the Rilli could be more easily and cheaply bridged than at the point where we crossed.

The right bank of the Lingtam at the crossing is a flat of considerable size, most of which has been cleared for cultivation. It is possible that the high hills which surround this level space may make it unhealthy at some seasons of the year; but should this not be the case, the place, in the event of a road being made, would probably become the chief halting-place between Rheinock and the upland pastures. Here we met some Thibetan traders, with their wives and families, on their way to Darjeeling. Their merchandise consisted of coarse blankets, which they meant to exchange for tobacco. They had spent six days in crossing from Choombi, travelling very slowly.

From the Lingtam we went along a rather uneven road, rising for the most part, to a place called Keu Laka, where we encamped for the night at an elevation of 5,654 feet, in a clearance near to the winter station of a family of herdsmen.

Herdsmen at Keu Laka.

These people belonged to a numerous class, who during the summer months live in the valley of the Mochoo, in Thibet, where they generally have some grain cultivation; but their chief support is derived from their flocks and herds, which they put out to graze on the great pastures which lie on both the Sikhim and Thibet sides of the Chola Range. When the snow begins to fall on the uplands, they drive their sheep and cattle to the lower slopes of Sikhim, where they cultivate patches of wheat, barley, and buckwheat. The family we saw at Keu Laka consisted of an old widow and her children and grandchildren, ten in number, besides servants. The old woman was clearly undisputed mistress of everything, although her sons were by no means young men; and it was pleasant to see the ready obedience that every one paid to her orders. We were told that there were over three hundred head of cattle in her herd, and I counted some seventy cows at milking time, all sleek and in good case, and many of them really handsome animals.

One of the old woman's sons told me that a good cow gives six quarts of milk daily, and that he valued such a cow at Rs. 34. He said that they supply butter and a kind of cream cheese to the Darjeeling market, as well as to those of Thibet, all of which, including Lassa, are mainly dependant for beef, as well as butter and cheese, on the produce of the herds of the Phari valley.

These herdsmen, as well as all the others I met in this part of Sikhim, paid revenue, both to the Rajah of Sikhim and to the Thibet Government, through the ex-Dewan Namgnay. The revenue is paid in kind—in butter and cheese—to the value of about Rs. 6 yearly to each Government; besides this, my informant said that they were liable to some other demands, both in kind and service, but that these last were occasional and not very heavy. He said, too, that they were sometimes compelled to sell a cow to the Sikhim Rajah or to a Phari Jungpen for less than the market value, and that they had from time to time to make presents to the Sikhim officials; but that this last item did not come heavy on account of the Rajah being near. On the whole, he did not consider that they were very badly off.

I found out afterwards that the herd of the old woman of Keu Laka was considered by no means an unusually large one in her part of Thibet, and that many persons own much greater numbers of cattle; while it is said to be not uncommon for a family to keep a flock of four or five thousand sheep.

On the 29th we left Keu Laka, at first descending some hundred feet by a very steep rocky path to a stream, which was crossed by a bridge of logs. Leaving the stream, we ascended another steep and rocky hill to a lovely glade in the temperate forest, at about 7,000 feet. From this glade we ascended still through the great oak forest to between 8,000 and 9,000 feet, when we got into heavy bamboo, called by my people "maling," which seemed to me the same as the "mooly" of the jungle of East Bengal. This part of the route, as is generally the case in bamboo jungle, was very difficult and fatiguing; but it would be quite easy to make a good road. After a tedious climb through bamboo, we came suddenly upon tree rhododendrons, which became more numerous, but smaller, as we got higher; until at last, when we reached the ridge, the bamboo had disappeared and was replaced by dwarf rhododendron.

After going some little way along the ridge, we found our camp pitched on an open, but rather uneven, patch of ground, called Jeyluk. Here I found Lasso Kazi, the Sikhim vakeel at Darjeeling, whom I had sent to Choombi some time before I started to inform the Rajah that I was coming. He now brought a letter from the Rajah, in which he said that his eldest sister, a nun at Choombi, was dangerously ill, and that his own health was bad; that the Phari Jungpens and Changzed would meet me near the Jeylep Pass; and that he would come

Jeyluk.

if I wished it, but hoped that I would excuse him on account of his own and his sister's health. I answered that I would not settle anything about a meeting with him till I had seen Changzed at the Pass.

Mount Lingtu.

Our road on the 30th, for some time after we left Jeyluk, rose gradually through bamboo and rhododendron till we came, at about 10,700 feet, to a level neck covered with juniper and other new vegetation, which connected the ridge we had been ascending with a steep pine-clad hill called Lingtu, which rises suddenly to a height of about 2,000 feet from the neck. The path goes up this hill, and though steep in some places, is far from being so difficult as it appears from below. I estimated the height of the point where the path crosses the hill to be more than 12,500 feet; but this is a mere guess, for the index hand of the aneroid had got fixed between 20 and 31 long before we got to the top. We had now got into the upland pastures, which extend to the foot of the Jeylep Pass,—a succession of low rolling hills, generally covered with scrub rhododendron, and slightly-depressed grassy valleys, with frequent patches of silver fir and occasional masses of rock covered with exquisitely-coloured mosses and lichen.

Gnatong.

We found very few cattle in the uplands through which we passed, but numerous unoccupied huts of herdsmen showed that these pastures are much frequented during the rains; and we could see with a glass immense herds grazing on a great expanse of grassy slopes and valleys some miles to our north, where are said to be the best pasturages in Sikhim.

Kophu.

We encamped on the night of the 30th in a wide grassy valley called Gnatong, and next day went on by an easy route over a comparatively level country to the foot of the Jeylep

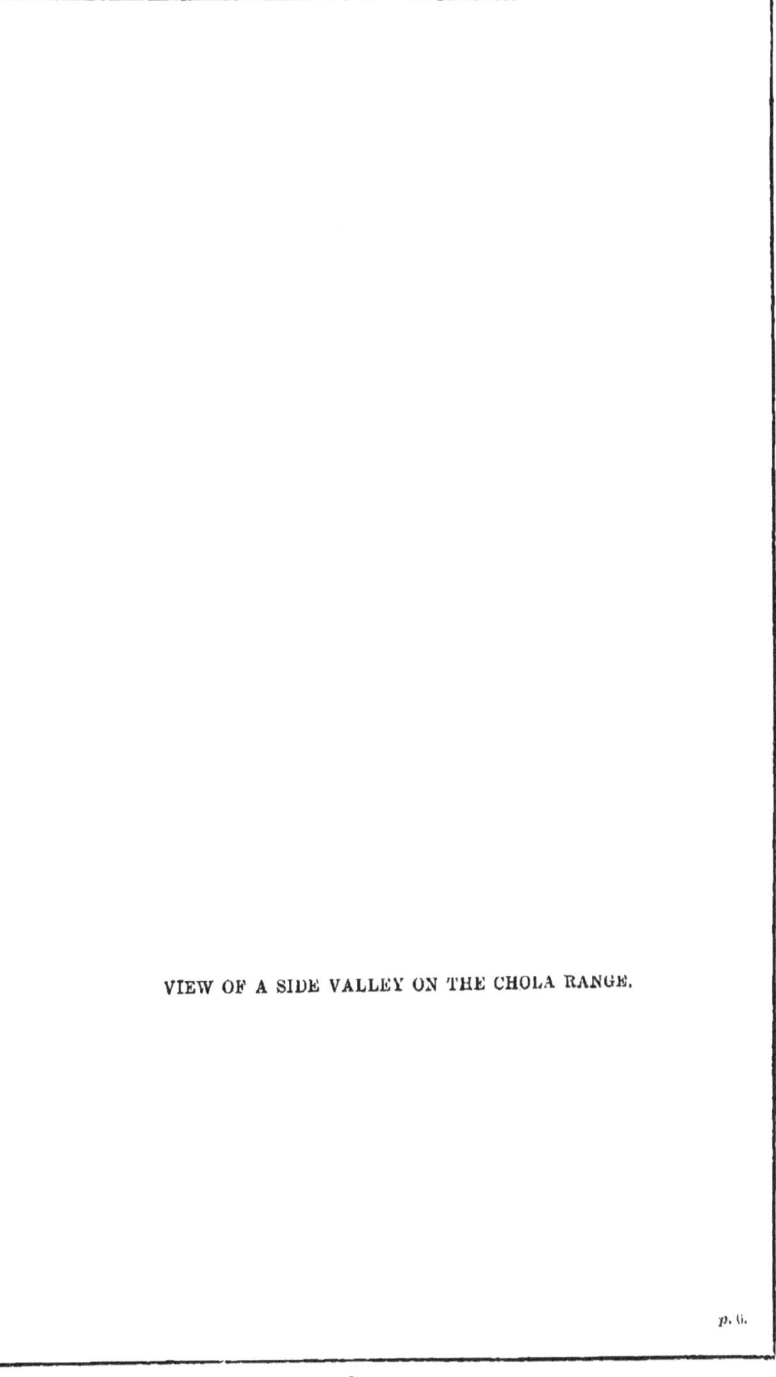

VIEW OF A SIDE VALLEY ON THE CHOLA RANGE.

Pass, where we encamped on the bank of a frozen stream flowing through a grassy and rather marshy valley called Kophu. Here we found messengers from Choombi awaiting our arrival, who said that Changzed and the ex-Dewan Namgnay were on their way from Choombi and would arrive at the Pass that evening, and that the Jungpen of Phari would arrive next day.

These messengers had been directed to ascertain whether I would allow the ex-Dewan Namgnay to cross the frontier, as he had been for ever excluded from Sikhim by the 7th Article of the Treaty of 1861. After some consideration, I decided that it would be well to receive him, as such meeting might give opportunities of finding out his exact position and influence, as well as his present sentiments towards our Government. Besides this, I had heard on all sides that, if he liked, he could give me more information on all subjects connected with Thibet than any one else. I therefore told the messengers to inform him that I was willing to receive him unofficially, and on my own responsibility, but that this did not in any way affect the prohibition contained in the treaty, which would still continue in full force, nor was my action to be in any way taken as an indication of any intention on the part of Government to condone his past offences.

The ex-Dewan.

I may say here that I was not disappointed in my hope of getting valuable information from him, for he supplied more than I obtained from all other sources together. He appeared to me to be a man of great mental and bodily activity, and an unusually quick intelligence. He showed a great eagerness for information, and a rare insight in grasping the meaning of subjects quite outside his own experience. But these qualities were counterbalanced by

His character.

a childish vanity, which he did not attempt to conceal, and which, coupled with a sanguine temperament, must make his judgment very unreliable in many important matters.

And position. Still, in spite of these drawbacks, he is on the whole the most considerable man with whom I have had dealings either on this or the North-East Frontier: and he has great weight in Thibet. This was evident from the respect paid to everything he said both by Changzed and the Phari Jungpens, over whom he exercises a kind of undefined authority, mainly based on his influence with the high officials of Lassa, and on the confidence which the latter place in his experience and knowledge of the affairs of the frontiers. But he is not Governor of Choombi, as has frequently been stated, and in fact has no recognized official position.

He has received a grant of land from the Dalai Lama and a high-class button through the Ampahs, or representatives of the Chinese Emperor at Lassa. In consideration of these favors he is supposed to give the Chechep Depen of Giantzi and the Jungpens of Phari the benefit of his advice when required. As far as I could judge from my intercourse with the ex-Dewan, he seemed very anxious to regain the favour of our Government, and I think that he really means to do us all the service in his power. He clearly sees that he has gained nothing by his former conduct, while probably he fancies that something is to be made by serving us now, and it was quite evident that he is exceedingly fond of gain.

I believe that much use might be made of him in our dealings with Thibet, if our frontier officers keep well in mind that his vanity will often lead him to promise more than it is in his power to perform, and that his hopefulness must always tend to make him underrate the difficulties of every undertaking.

Arrival of Changzed, the Dewan, and the Jungpens.

After the messengers left, Thibetans came pouring down from the Pass, with tents made of yaks' hair and canvas, ponies, flocks of sheep, and provisions of various kinds; and in a wonderfully short time a considerable encampment had sprung up on the opposite side of the stream to ours. The Rajah sent a durbar tent for me, which in shape, arrangement, and even in ornament, bore a curious resemblance to the great marble Audience Halls in the palaces of Delhi and Agra. In the afternoon Changzed and the Dewan arrived in their camp. As they had come that day all the way from Choombi, and it was getting very cold, I put off receiving them till the next morning.

Soon after this a telegram from the Lieutenant-Governor, recalling Major Lindsay, whose services were required to commence the Northern Bengal Railway, came in, having been forwarded by express. Major Lindsay determined to start next morning, to my great regret; for I lost in him a pleasant companion at the time when I most wanted his aid in the survey of the Passes.

The Jungpens of Phari arrived early on the morning of the 1st, or rather one Jungpen and a subordinate who acted as the representative of the other, said to be absent in Lassa.

Interviews with Changzed.

About 10 A.M. I received Changzed and the Dewan. I told them that I had been sent to convey the orders of Government upon the points raised in the memorial submitted by the Rajah to the Lieutenant-Governor when at Darjeeling. I said that, as I understood my instructions, I was bound to communicate

the orders to the Rajah in person; but that I
was very unwilling to ask him to come into
tents on the Jeylep at this inclement season,
particularly as he was said to be in great
sorrow about his sister. I said that I was quite
willing to go to him at Choombi, but pointed
out that, as I had already informed them, I
had been distinctly forbidden by Government
to cross the frontier without special invitation
from the Thibetan authorities. I suggested
that they should use their influence with the
Phari Jungpens to procure me such an invitation, and in this way save the Rajah the trouble
of coming to meet me. They promised to
try; but said that they had little hope of
success, as the Jungpens had been sent for the
purpose of preventing me from crossing the
frontier.

And with the Jungpens.

They then went away and returned about two
hours after with the Jungpen and his associate,
whom I shall call the Deputy Jungpen. The
former is a young man, tall and very stout,
with a heavy unprepossessing face; but his
manner was remarkably good. It was cour-
teous, dignified, and at the same time perfectly
unaffected. His voice was pleasant, and he
spoke in a quiet, refined tone. Altogether, he
gave me the idea of a man accustomed to live
in a society which had acquired a considerable
amount of cultivation. He is said to be the
son of a highly-placed Thibetan official, and to
have spent some years in the bureaus of Lassa
and Jigatzi. He was appointed to Phari about
a year ago, and it was his first independent
charge of importance. The Deputy Jungpen, though richly dressed and entitled to
wear a button, evidently belonged to a much
lower class,—not differing very much from the
ignorant and unpolished Bhooteas of Sikhim
and Bhootan whom we are accustomed to meet.

His opinion, as representing the absent Jungpen, was occasionally asked for in a formal way, but he never volunteered an observation; and in all our interviews he took up, in a marked way, a position of inferiority to Changzed, the Jungpen, and ex-Dewan.

After some conversation on indifferent subjects, I told the Jungpens that there were several questions which I wished to discuss with them; but that I must first settle about a meeting with the Sikhim Rajah, which was the main object of my visit. I repeated to them what I had already said to Changzed and the Dewan, and asked them to consult with them and decide on the best thing to be done. The Jungpen answered, with much circumlocution and many compliments, that he was very sorry that he could not give me the necessary invitation to Choombi, as he had received special instructions from the Ampahs to meet me on the frontier, to hear all that I wished to say, and to report it to Lassa; but at the same time to explain to me that there was an agreement between Thibet and China that no foreigner should cross the frontier, and that no European had ever been allowed into Thibet. I said that, as regards the invitation, I wished him to settle that matter with the Sikhim people; but that he was mistaken in saying that no European had visited Thibet.

I then told him about the missions of Bogle and Turner, and showed him Turner's sketch of the Tisshoo Lama's tomb, which he professed not to recognize. The ex-Dewan took the book to look at the picture, which however seemed to convey no idea to his mind. But when on turning over the leaves he came accidentally on the picture of the temple called Kugopea, he at once exclaimed, with evident surprise, that he recognized it, and said that

Objections to my crossing the frontier.

Turner's sketch accurately represents the present appearance of the building. The Jungpen was obliged to allow that this was the case, and seemed somewhat disconcerted at first; but, after thinking for a little time, he said that though he had never heard of Turner's mission, he supposed he had been in Thibet; but that I stated that it is almost one hundred years since the date of his visit, while the present arrangement had been made by Kishen, the Tongtong (or Prince) of the Chinese Empire, who had been sent to settle the affairs of Thibet less than thirty years ago. In answer to some questions of mine, the Jungpen explained that by an arrangement between Kishen and the Thibetan authorities, the direct management of frontier affairs had been committed to the Ampahs, and that at the same time it was settled that there should be no intercourse between Thibet and British India; and, above all, that no Europeans should be allowed to cross the Thibetan frontier. He then said that I, as an official, would understand that all he could do was to obey orders, whether he approved of them or not.

Before this Changzed and the Dewan made an attempt to persuade the Jungpen, as I afterwards understood, that the orders of the Ampahs were not so positive as to prevent their taking me to Choombi, on the plea that I had been directed by my Government to meet the Rajah there. The Jungpen, on hearing this, said to me that if I considered myself bound by my orders to go to Choombi, he would not oppose me, but that the results would be his absolute ruin,—a rupture between Sikhim and Thibet, and no improvement in our relations with the latter state. He added that the Sikhim durbar were well aware of this, and that the Ampahs had written to the Rajah on the subject. I again explained that I had received distinct orders not

Alleged engagements with the Chinese.

to go into Thibet without an express invitation, but that I was also bound to meet the Sikhim Rajah. The Jungpen offered to report the matter to his immediate superior, the Chechep Depen at Giantzi, and ask for his instructions. I put off giving any answer to this proposition till next day, as I wished, before settling anything, to find out the exact nature of the letter from the Ampahs to the Sikhim Rajah which the Jungpen had alluded to.

Next morning I rode to the Jeylep Pass, accompanied by the Dewan and the Deputy Jungpen. The boundary was marked by several cairns of stones, on one of which was an oblong board with a Thibetan inscription on one side stating that it showed the point where the boundary between Sikhim and Thibet crossed the Jeylep Pass. Above was a large red oblong seal, said to be that of a Chinese official at Giantzi, and below two small seals, one of which I think was that of the Sikhim Rajah. On the other side of the board was an inscription in the Chinese character which no one with me could read. *[The Jeylep Pass.]*

On my way back I stopped at Changzed's tent. He had got breakfast for me, consisting of precisely the same dishes as those described by Mr. Blanford, in his narrative published in the *Journal of the Asiatic Society*, Part II, No. 4, of 1871. The Phari Jungpens were not present at breakfast, and I had a long unrestrained talk with Changzed and the Dewan about Thibetan politics. They were clearly of opinion that the main hindrance to free intercourse with that country is the Chinese policy of exclusiveness; but they said that hitherto this had coincided with a feeling in the minds of the Thibet officials that it was safer to have nothing to do with us. *[Breakfast with Changzed.]*

Of late, however, there has been a movement in favour of abandoning the policy of isolation, and the Dewan said that at the present time some of the leading officials are agitating in that direction; but he added that anything of this kind takes a long time in Thibet, and that it is very difficult to advance without the co-operation of the Ampahs. Both he and Changzed urged strongly the advisability of getting a declaration from the Government of Pekin that the obstacles now put in the way of free intercourse are unauthorized. They said that this would strengthen the hands of the party favorable to a change of policy, while it would deprive their opponents of their great argument against innovation.

I gathered that much uneasiness was felt in Thibet at the attitude of Sir Jung Bahadoor and the threats of the Nepalese, and that in consequence the Dalai Lama and his advisers had made up their dispute with the Ampahs, and were very anxious to stand well with China.

Letter from the Chinese Ampahs at Lassa.

I asked Changzed whether it was true that the Ampahs had written to the Rajah about my visit, as the Jungpen had said. He said it was true, and, after a little hesitation, produced a letter from a bundle of papers.

It was written in the Thibetan language and character, on fine Daphne paper, and had a large oblong red seal at foot, the device on which was different from that on the board I had seen at the Pass. It was said to be the official seal of the Ampahs. The letter was contained in an enormous envelope of China paper, highly scented with musk, and covered with red seals like that on the letter, and with Chinese characters, under which were translations in Thibetan. I subsequently got this letter with considerable difficulty from the Sikhim people, who were much afraid that they might get into trouble if we made any use of it at Pekin. Both letter and envelope will accompany this report, but I give the following translation of the letter, as it is important:—

Translation of letter.

"By order of our master, the Emperor of China, we the Ampahs Jaw-lo-tin and Tin (*a*) address you, the Sikhim Rajah, the four Kalons (*b*) having made known to us the representation addressed to the Dalai Lama Rimbochay through the Chechep Depen of Giantzi, Gempo Pinchow, by you conjointly with the Jungpens of Phari, Undee Durjee, and Minjur Durjee, dated the 4th day of the month Dow Dimpo, and forwarded by horse express. In this it was stated that you had a meeting with the Peling Lord Sahib (*c*) during the month Dow Napho at Darjeeling, and that he requested you to have the roads through Sikhim repaired during the 10th month, as a Commissioner Sahib and a Deputy Commissioner Sahib would visit the frontier during the 8th and 9th months (*d*). It was also stated that these officers would proceed to Rinchingong and Choombi unless met on the frontier by you, the Phari Jungpens, and Dewan Namgnay.

"You furthermore promised a full report of the proposed interview.

(*a.*) In original "The Pho-to-thong Ampahs Jaw-lo-tin and Tin." According to another reading, Pho-to-thong and Jaw-lo-tin are the names of the Ampahs; some of my interpreters taking Pho-to-thong as a title of both Ampahs, others taking it to be the name of one of them.

(*b.*) Kalon is the Chinese term for the four Secretaries of the Government of Lassa, called Shaffes in Thibetan; the latter term is the one best known here, but the former title is that used by Huc.

(*c.*) "Peling" was the word used to describe the English by the Thibetans who talked with Huc.

(*d.*) There is here clearly a mistake of the copyist of the letter. The meaning intended must have been to prepare the roads during the 8th and 9th months (*i.e.*, August and September) for the visit to be made in the 10th month.

"On receipt of this letter we, in consultation with the Thibet officials, took into consideration the question whether the Peling Lord Sahib did or did not express the wishes attributed to him by you, and we came to the conclusion that, according to the golden writing of the Emperor of China, and the arrangement which has hitherto existed and which we have sworn to maintain, the Peling Sahibs should not be allowed to cross the frontier (a).

"You should explain all this to the Sahibs, and do all in your power to persuade them to return without entering Thibet. In case you should be successful, there will be no need of the Phari Jungpens going to meet them. But should you fail to induce the Sahibs to return, then the Phari Jungpens should go to the frontier and explain to them that it would be contrary to custom for them to cross the frontier, and that it is, as it were, a matter of life and death for us to uphold the existing arrangements.

"But they should do all this in such a manner as not to give offence, and should do nothing which could possibly give rise to complications in the future.

"You should report at once the result of the steps taken; and if on this, or any future occasion, the Sahibs should insist on crossing the frontier, immediate and frequent reports should be made to us through the Chechep Depen of Giantzi.

"Your State of Sikhim borders on Thibet: you know what is in our minds, and what our policy is; you are bound to prevent the Peling Sahibs from crossing the frontier; yet

---

(a.) This passage appears a little obscure in the original. I have had four independent translations made of it, all of which differ more or less; but the one given above seems most nearly to represent the meaning.

it is entirely through your action in making roads for the Sahibs through Sikhim that they are going to make the projected attempt.

"If you continue to behave in this manner, it will not be well with you.

"In future you should fulfil your obligations and obey the orders of the Dalai Lama Rimbochay and the twelfth Emperor of China (a).

"Dated the Thibetan year Choojah, the eighth month, the eleventh day of the month, corresponding with August 1873."

On hearing the contents of this letter, which seemed to me authentic, I began to think that I might do most to further my great object of establishing free intercourse with Thibet by giving up all idea of crossing the frontier during this visit. It seemed probable that I should not gain much by going to Choombi, while I might lose the opportunity of urging upon the Jungpens, and through them on the higher Thibet officials, the arguments against the policy of isolation which they have adopted.

Idea of going to Choombi given up.

Finally, I came to the conclusion that this was the right course to take, and I told Changzed that I did not wish him to press the Jungpens any further for an invitation to Choombi, but that he should arrange at once for the Rajah to meet me at his own side of the frontier at such place and time as might be most convenient to him. I then asked to have the Jungpens sent for, as they had already said that they had not brought a tent fit to receive me in. When they came, I told them that I had settled that the Sikhim Rajah

Conversation with the Jungpens.

(a.) That is, twelfth of the existing or Tsing dynasty. According to our lists, Kitsiang is only the eighth Emperor of his dynasty.

was to come to meet me, and that I had given up any idea I had of going to Choombi. The Jungpen seemed greatly relieved at hearing this, and said he was sorry that his orders had not allowed him to invite me across the frontier, again repeating that I, as an official, could understand his position.

I then said that Government, not having anticipated my meeting with any Thibetan officials, had not given me any instructions concerning such a meeting, and that therefore anything I might say to him had not the authority of my Government, but was merely the opinion of an experienced official about its views and wishes. Under this explanation I requested him to report what I should say in full to his superiors.

Concerning trade.

He said that he had received instructions to make a full report, but that of course he could not accept or reject any proposition which I might make. I then said that one of the objects of my visit was to inquire into the question connected with the trade between our territories and Thibet, and that I meant to recommend strongly the construction of a road through Sikhim, under our treaty with that State, as well as some other measures which I thought likely to encourage trade; but I said that I should also take occasion to bring prominently to the notice of Government that, while the majority of our subjects are not allowed to enter Thibet for the purpose of trade, crowds of Thibetans are constantly pouring into our bazaars.

Our Government, I said, was very glad to have these traders come in, and did what it could to protect and encourage them, and I thought it but fair that the Thibetan Government should treat our people in the same way.

This exclusion seemed the more indefensible since people of Cashmere, Nepal, Sikhim, and Bhootan—States dependant on, or allied with us—were freely admitted.

The conversation which followed on this subject led to some allusion to our policy with regard to Himalayan States. I described this as the encouragement of trade to the utmost of our power, and the maintenance of strong friendly States along our frontier. In support of this I instanced our treatment of Afghanistan, Cashmere, and Nepal, and said that I did not pretend that the policy was a purely unselfish one; that of course we were glad when other States were prosperous; but that we ourselves derived great advantages from the neighbourhood of strong, friendly, and flourishing States.

Our policy towards Himalayan States.

In the first place, I said, large classes of our people are manufacturers or traders, and it is an object of great importance to find markets for their goods. But it is a matter of far greater moment that there should be powerful, well-organized, and friendly States to preserve order along the long and difficult northern frontier which we do not want to hold ourselves, but which without such States would be an intolerable nuisance to the defenceless low lands. By keeping the peace along this frontier, such States fully repay our support and occasional aid, while prospering greatly themselves. I pointed out that Thibet is now practically the only considerable State on the frontier that is not on such a friendly footing with us and benefiting thereby, and asked the Jungpen to contrast the result of the policy of isolation in Thibet with that of the opposite policy as carried out by Sir Jung Bahadoor's government in Nepal.

Relations of Thibet with Nepal.

The Jungpen, who had shown throughout by his questions and remarks that he took an intelligent interest in what I was saying, acknowledged that the relative positions of Nepal and Thibet had become very unsatisfactory, and asked me, with much appearance of anxiety, whether I had any late intelligence of the intentions of Sir Jung Bahadoor, and how he had received a proposal which had been made some time previously that he should send Commissioners to the frontier to meet some Thibet officials. I said that he had refused to send Commissioners to the frontier, and had declared that the Thibetans must go to Khatmandoo if they wished to make any answer to the complaints of the Nepali representative at Thibet. This news evidently was not expected by the Jungpen, and it seemed to make him very uncomfortable. He said that the people of Thibet would do much to avoid a rupture with Nepal, for they were quite aware that the resources of the latter State had increased greatly of late; but that they feared that Sir Jung Bahadoor was determined to attack them, in which case they would fight to the last. The British Government, added the Jungpen, might confer a great benefit on Thibet by using its influence to moderate the aggressive policy of Nepal. I answered that I knew our Government to be anxious to have peace maintained on the frontier, and to be of use to its neighbours when possible; but that, for my own part, I could not see how it could interfere between Nepal and Thibet. If differences should arise between Bhootan and Nepal, or Sikhim and Nepal, our Government would certainly mediate between the two, and in all probability effectually; but a dispute between Nepal and Thibet is quite another matter. It appeared to me that our Government would not be justified in interfering unasked between a friendly State and one that refuses to have any relations with us. And, further, that even if our Government were to interfere, it could only hear the Nepal version of the dispute, and probably this would show Thibet to be altogether wrong and Nepal worthy of our support.

I took occasion in this connection again to dwell on the injury to Thibet caused by the policy of isolation. The Jungpen said that many people in Thibet had begun to distrust its soundness. For his own part, he considered it his duty to carry out orders without inquiry, whether they were good or bad; but he would repeat all that I had said to the Chechep Depen of Giantzi. I said that I was very sorry not to have met the Depen this time; but that it would probably be necessary for me, or some other officer of Government, to visit the frontier next year, possibly before the rains, as I did not see my way to settling finally all the matters about which I had come. In this case I hoped that a meeting with the Depen could be arranged, and I begged the Jungpen to tell this to the Depen. He said he would do so, but took care to explain that it was not in his power to give any promise that would bind the Depen.

On my return to camp I received a large present of sheep, blankets, butter, flour, salt, &c., from the Jungpens, to whom I gave in return a small musical box and a pair of binoculars. In the evening, as generally happened, a great number of people from the Phari Valley collected about my camp-fire and talked about roads, trade, their crops, and flocks, and herds, and other such matters. They went away earlier than usual; but after a little while some of the elders came back, and after making sure that none of the Jungpen's people were hanging about, asked me when we were going to take possession of the Phari Valley.

Conversation with Thibetan traders about annexation.

They were wearied, they said, of the oppressions of the officials, and having seen, when on their way to Darjeeling to trade, the prosperity of the countries which we had taken from Bhootan and Sikhim, they were anxious that we should at once annex their country, as they had heard we meant to do eventually. I told them that we had not the slightest intention of taking their country; that it was in the highest degree improbable that we should be compelled to do so; that we were very anxious to do what we could to help them by encouraging trade, making roads and bridges, and establishing marts; but that more than this we could not do. They then went away. My people seemed convinced that these people had made this inquiry of themselves; that there is a general belief that we shall eventually annex these Himalayan valleys; and that their inhabitants greatly desired that we should do so: but I am strongly inclined to suspect that the men were instigated by the Jungpens, with a view to sounding me, and finding out if there were ulterior motives for my visit; and, in a subsequent conversation, I took an opportunity of telling the Jungpens of our great unwillingness to extend our frontiers in any direction, and of explaining some of the chief objections to such extension towards the Himalayas.

Conversation with Changzed about the orders of Government.

On the morning of the 3rd, Changzed came across to my camp and had a long interview with me, in which I explained to him the orders of Government and discussed fully the different matters which I meant to take up formally when I had a meeting with the Rajah. I pointed out to him the conditions on which the increase of pension had been granted, and said that I relied on all the Sikhim officials supporting the Rajah in complying with them.

I told him that I was inclined to recommend the construction of a road over Jeyluk to the Jeylep, but that I should not make up my mind until I had explored the remaining Passes. He said that he thought I should find the route to the foot of Jeylep and the Pass itself far easier than any other line, and that if a road were decided on they would help in its construction to the best of their ability. He took up warmly the proposition of establishing a mart somewhere on the frontier, but objected to the sites proposed by me as being remote from the inhabited parts of Sikhim and too near the snows. He urged strongly the advantages of Guntuck, where he said the Rajah had long contemplated building a house, and where there was much level land, with plenty of water, in a perfect climate, neither too cold nor too hot. I promised to visit Guntuck on my way back, and to mention in my report that the Sikhim durbar wished to have the mart established there.

I explained to him fully the plan on which it is proposed to start the Bhootea Boarding School at Darjeeling, for the teaching of English, Thibetan, and hill-surveying. He expressed the most unqualified approval of the idea, and said that he would undertake that it should be attended by several young and promising boys belonging to families of influence in Sikhim. He was particularly pleased that hill-surveying was to be taught; and I may mention in this connection, that while we were at Pemiongchi, some of the Lamas at that monastery told Major Judge, R.E., that they wished to learn surveying. Changzed promised to send his hare-lipped brother to Darjeeling. He said that the boy would be accompanied by his mother, and that he would have come this cold weather if it had not been for the illness of the elder sister, which had thrown everything into confusion.

Talk with the Dewan.

After much more talk Changzed went away, and the Dewan brought me a pile of letters, which he said would prove that he was not the chief person concerned in the detention of Doctors Campbell and Hooker. I refused to look at his letters, and told him that I could not hold out to him the slightest hope that Government would consent to re-open the question of his past conduct; but I said that there might be some possibility of his obtaining forgiveness by future good service. I added that I was willing to believe that he was anxious to serve us, and even that during the last few months he had been working hard; but I pointed out that there were no results of this work which I could lay before Government as proof that he had earned forgiveness. I then told him that I could not permit him to be present when I met the Rajah in durbar. He said that all he asked now was that I should believe that he was anxious for forgiveness, and resolved to serve us faithfully and to the best of his ability in future. In proof of this, he said that he meant to go to both Jigatzi and Lassa, and represent, in the strongest manner he could, to all his friends among the high officials and to the Dalai Lama himself, all the arguments which I had urged against the policy of isolation.

Changzed, the Jungpens, and Dewan dine with me.

After this Changzed and the Jungpens, whom I had asked to dinner, came over. The real Jungpen, Changzed, and the Dewan, sat at table with me; the Deputy Jungpen on a rug spread on the ground. The Jungpen, who of course had never seen a knife and fork before, took everything as a matter of course, as a well-bred man of the world, and made wonderfully few mistakes; Changzed, very curious about everything, but more afraid of making solecisms, carefully watched me and imitated me in everything. The Dewan, who acted the part of parasite to perfection, went into most amusing rapture about all he saw. He admired my table appointments, which were in truth a very rough camp assortment, as the perfection of refined convenience. The biscuits far excelled anything that could be procured in Thibet, and could scarcely be equalled in China; the meats were such as are rarely tasted, except at the table of an Ampah newly arrived at Lassa. From time to time he called the attention of his fellow-guests to some delicacy or elegance which seemed to him to have escaped their notice.

Instead of wine I gave them tea, without milk or sugar, having the cups constantly refilled after their fashion. It was Darjeeling tea, and they agreed, I think sincerely, that tea of such quality could not be bought at Lassa, and that it was superior to any imported from China, except perhaps some sent from time to time by the Emperor to the Dalai Lama for his own use. They said that the prohibition on the import of Indian tea is entirely due to the Ampahs, and let it appear pretty clearly that this part of the Chinese policy is not popular with Thibet officials.

After dinner I showed them a photographic album, which I had filled with cartes of the Queen, Royal Family, and various prominent public men in England and India, and a revolving stereoscope, with fifty views of public buildings and landscapes in Great Britain. I had a description of each photograph written over it in Thibetan. My guests showed great interest in these pictures. I was somewhat amused to remark that the Jungpen evidently fixed upon the Duke of Argyle and Mr. Grant Duff as the real rulers

Photographs; stereoscopic views.

of India, and looked upon them as of greater practical importance than the Queen and the Viceroy. Indeed, he seemed to look upon the rank of the Duke of Argyll and his connection with the Royal House as presumptions against his political importance, and to believe that the work must be done by, and therefore the power rest with, Mr. Grant Duff. The Dewan, who had seen the stereoscopic views on a previous day, explained them to the Jungpens, and in doing so showed that he really understood what the pictures represented. They were all much interested in the views of cathedrals and churches, the size and splendour of which they seemed to think were indications of the greatness and piety of the nation.

Before the Jungpen left, I again spoke to him about the desirability of free intercourse and unimpeded trade between our respective countries, and he once more promised to report what I had said to him to the Chechep Depen, and to inform that officer of my desire that he should meet me or any one that might be deputed to visit the frontier next year.

Arrival of the Sikhim Rajah, and my meeting with him.

That evening we heard that the Rajah had left Choombi, and would arrive at Kophu next morning, and that his sister was in a hopeless state, scarcely expected to survive till his return to Choombi. I therefore settled with Changzed that I should see the Rajah immediately on his arrival, and communicate to him the orders of Government without any delay. He arrived on the forenoon of the 4th, and I went over when I heard that he was ready to receive me. He was evidently in deep distress; but received me in a friendly manner, and inquired with some appearance of interest about my journey, and whether I had been assisted by his people, as he had directed. I thanked him for all the attention which had been shown, which I promised to bring to the notice of Government. I then informed him that Government had increased his pension to Rs. 12,000 per annum, and explained the conditions on which the increase had been granted. He assured me that it was his earnest desire to comply with all the wishes of Government. After having briefly mentioned the different points in which we wished for their co-operation, I said that I had fully discussed all details with Changzed, and that now, unless he wished, I should not trouble him in his present sorrow by asking for more than his general confirmation of the promises made by Changzed. He said that I might accept anything said by Changzed as coming from himself, and that he felt himself bound by any promises made by the Minister.

Changzed, who had been present, then went away, and I was about to go; but the Rajah would not let me till I had eaten with him. When, however, he tried to eat some food which had been laid before us, he fairly broke down, quite over-mastered by his grief. It seemed to me that there was something very touching in the intense sorrow shown by this ordinarily stolid old man, whom we have scarcely credited with any human feeling. I asked him when he meant to return to Choombi. He said that he would return my visit next day, and hoped that I would let him go away on the day after. I said that I would dispense with the return visit, and that he might go next day if he wished. He seemed grateful for this, and settled to go, and I promised to ride up to the Pass with him and see him off. I said that I should not fail to represent to Government the circumstances under which he had come to meet me, and at his request I gave him permission to remain this year at Choombi, while Changzed and the young brother were to go to Tumlong.

Final interview with Changzed.

Changzed returned with me to my camp, and we had another long talk about the matters previously discussed, and among other things about the dispute between Bhootan and Sikhim. He seemed very anxious to make out that the real cause of quarrel is the anger felt by Bhootan at the friendly relations between our Government and Sikhim, and he avoided in a remarkable way the question of the Tassiding Lama. I had several times previously observed this unwillingness on the part of the Sikhim Durbar to discuss this subject, and their desire to make out that the interference of the Deb Rajah was merely an excuse for annoying Sikhim, while I had reason to suspect that the dispute in reality involved a question of spiritual jurisdiction. I therefore resolved to visit Pemiongchi and Tassiding on my way back, and learn what I could on the spot.

I had received considerable presents from the Sikhim people,—a pair of yaks, three mules, a pony, a large flock of sheep, blankets, flour, butter, salt, &c.; and I now gave, as return presents, a large musical-box to the Rajah, a revolver to Changzed, and some other things to the rest of the family. I gave the revolving stereoscope to the Dewan, who said that he would take it to Lassa and exhibit it there. I shall submit a detailed account of these presents when I have disposed of those received by me. Changzed hurried off that afternoon for Choombi, on getting still worse accounts of his sister's condition. The Jungpens had already left for Giantzi, to make their report to the Depen and to one of the

Ampahs, who was expected to arrive there a few days later.

Next morning I started with the Rajah to accompany him to the Pass; but as he was in a litter, the bearers of which went very slowly, and as I feared that a heavy mass of clouds, which was drifting up from the south-west, might shut out the view of the Phari Valley, I rode on ahead and waited for the Rajah at the Pass. When he came up, he got out of his litter, and we exchanged white silk scarfs with many expressions of friendliness. The Rajah showed great anxiety lest I should be caught in snow, and begged of me to hasten down to the warmer parts of Sikhim. He then went down the hill; I was left with my people on the Pass without a single Thibetan in sight. The view over the valley was very fine. Chumalari, on the north-north-east, rose far above all the other peaks, though there were three snow-capped peaks on the same ridge further east, apparently of great height. South of Chumalari was another great range running nearly east and west, the most conspicuous and only snow-peak of which was Pemla, or Temla, on the Bhootan boundary. The Mochoo rises between these two ridges, and flows for some way in a westerly direction, possibly with a little northing, passing Phari on, I understand, its left bank. Some time after this it takes a turn to the south, flowing round the Pemla range, and having on its right bank at this part of its course a great slope, on which are situated the monastery and villages of Killoomsi. In its southerly course it now passes by Choombi and the great monastery and village of Rinchingong, and so under the Jeylep Pass into Bhootan, through a Pass which is much used as a road between the two countries. Paro is said to be three days' journey from

Description of the Jeylep Pass.

Rinchingong by this route, which is described as better than the one over Pemla taken by Turner.

A few feet below the Pass on the Thibet side was a small frozen lake, the waters of which drain into the Mochoo by a stream flowing through dense fir-woods, which seem to grow at a much higher elevation on the Thibet side than they do to the west of the Chola range. A few hundred feet lower down, on a hill to the north-east, was an extensive monastery, said to be dependent on that of Rinchingong. This monastery is said to have been once very flourishing, but to have declined owing to a prolonged and violent contest for the chair of Head Lama between rival claimants, one of whom was a native of Bhootan and the other a native of Sikhim. The dispute was finally settled by the Dalai Lama in favour of the Bhootanese, as I have been informed; but Dr. Campbell, in his generally accurate account of the Choombi Valley, contributed to the Royal Asiatic Society, says that the decision was in favour of the Sikhim man. I should think that the elevation of the Pass is about 14,000 feet, and that it is not 1,000 feet higher than Kophu. The road up is remarkably easy. Even in its present state it may be ridden both up and down, except for a short distance not far from the Pass. The gradient is very slight, except at the place just referred to, where there is a steep rise of a couple of hundred feet. The first part from Kophu runs along the bank of a stream flowing from the Pass, and rises almost imperceptibly; then comes the sharp rise, and then a gentle ascent leading up to the Pass. There would be little difficulty in making a carriage road the whole way.

On my return to camp I sent for the Dewan, and got a great mass of information from him about Thibet. After which I let him go, on his promising to come to meet me at the Chola, if I should think of any further questions to put to him.

Next morning I started for the Gnatui Pass. For a little way the route lay along the level plain of Kophu in a northerly direction; but then went down a very steep descent, for perhaps a thousand feet, into a fir-clad valley, in which was a long lake called the Nemitzo. I do not think that I have seen anything in India so beautiful as this gorge, with its lake surrounded by hills covered with fir-wood, and partly-frozen streams falling over precipices through a network of ice tracery. There are many similar valleys between the comparatively level uplands of this part of Sikhim. They form very singular features in the landscape, looking from a distance like huge earthquake-rents in the grassy plains. From the valley we had a stiff climb to the flat on the other side, which was more than usually marshy, with a large sheet of water fringed with sedge in the middle. My coolies went along the west side of this marsh to Sharab, where I meant to encamp, while I took a path leading in a north-easterly direction to the Gnatui Pass. Two Thibetans, who had been directed by the Jungpens to put up at each Pass a board similar to the one I saw at Jeylep, accompanied me and acted as guides. After leaving the marsh my route lay for some distance over low grassy hills, dotted with the abandoned stone huts of herdsmen who had taken their cattle to the lower hills for the winter. Then we went along the south face of the range to the north of the Pass, occasionally finding some difficulty in getting along the edge of landslips. In some places the ascent was rather steep, but I do not think that the Pass is very much higher than Jeylep;

Visit the Gnatui Pass.

but it is said to be more snowy, and I was shown a high cylinder of stone in the centre of the Pass, put up as a guide to travellers at times when the track is covered with snow. The view of the Phari Valley is much less extensive than that from Jeylep, but it gives one a better idea of the villages and cultivation about Choombi. A rather considerable stream flows from the Gnatui to the Mochoo, or Ammochoo, near Rinchingong.

Sikhim traders.

While we were at the Pass, a man from Guntuck, with his wife, came up with murwa of their own growing to the value of about six rupees, which they were taking to Choombi for sale. They said that they meant to take the proceeds to Phari, where they would buy salt, which they would bring in to Darjeeling, where they might probably lay out the proceeds of its sale in an investment for the Thibet market, if they found time to do so before next year's sowing season. I mention this case, as it is a typical one. There was scarce a day during my stay in East Sikhim that I did not meet people either coming from, or on their way to, Darjeeling with goods, the value of which at first sight seemed quite disproportioned to the labour that had to be undergone in taking them to market; but I have no doubt they find the traffic pays them. These merwa-sellers expected to get six rupees for their merwa at Choombi, and with this sum to be able to buy at Phari four maunds of salt, which they could sell in Darjeeling for Rs. 32, while the value of their murwa at Guntuck was only Rs. 4-8.

Camp at Sharab.

The first part of our return route from the Gnatui followed the road by which we had ascended; but before we got to the marsh we turned off to the north-west, and took a difficult and bad path running along the edge of a

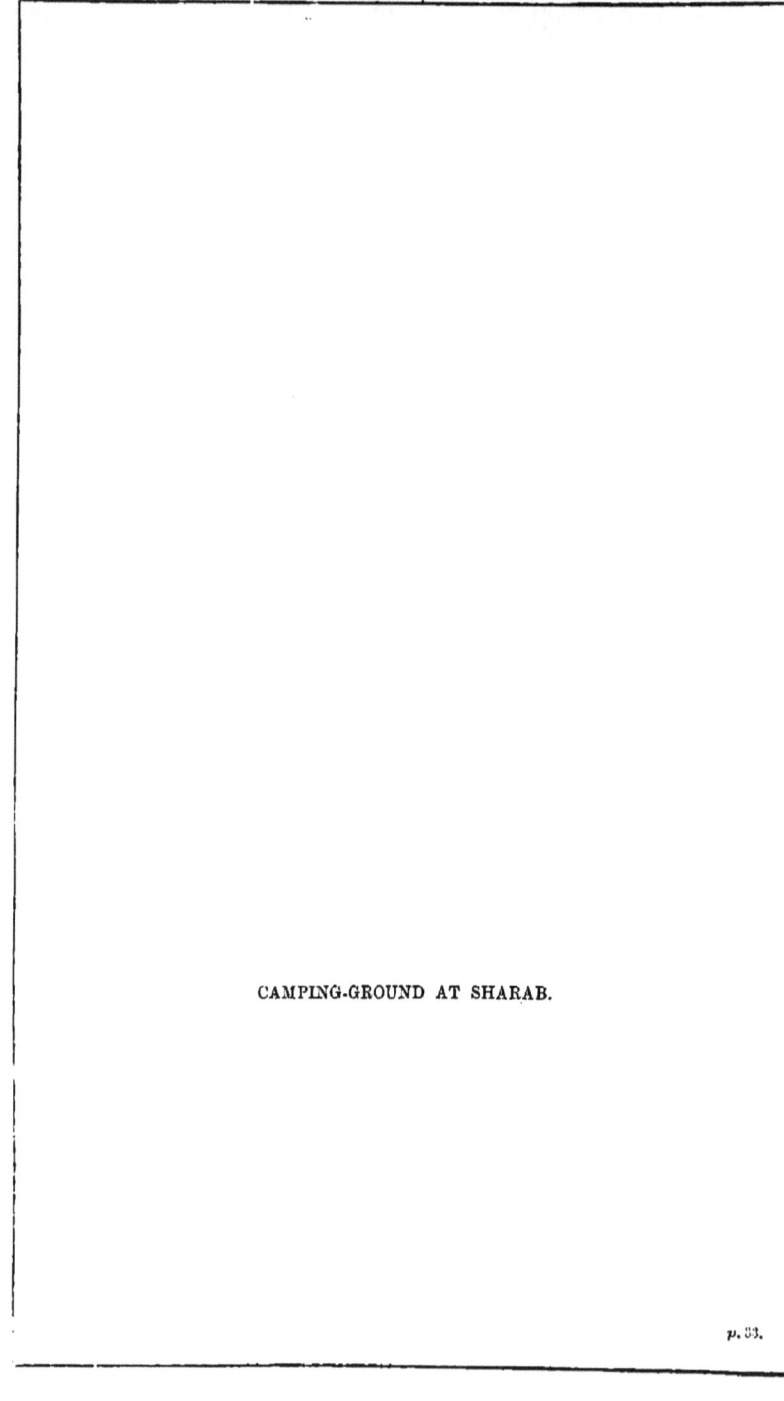

CAMPING-GROUND AT SHARAB.

precipitous ravine resembling the one we had crossed in the morning. On the way we passed a cave in which some very poor Thibetan traders, on their way to Darjeeling, were encamped for the night. After this we ascended continuously to Sharab, where I found our tents pitched at an elevation of under 14,000 feet, according to my estimate. Major Judge, R.E., however, who visited the place some days later, thinks that the height of our camp was not less than 15,000 feet. When I got into camp the weather looked very threatening,—the west wind, which had blown as usual throughout the day, having driven up huge masses of clouds; but as evening fell, the wind made its customary change to the east and dispersed the clouds, leaving a clear starry sky and intense frost.

Next morning I ascended to the Yakla, sending my coolies round to the place fixed for our encampment by a lower and shorter route. I went up a very picturesque valley, in which were a succession of glacier lakes, which seemed clearly to be portions of the bed of a torrent dammed up by moraines. In the valley I found some ripe seeds of the giant rhubarb, which I had previously searched for in vain, as all the plants about the Gnatui and Jeylep Passes had seeded and died down in October. Some parts of the ascent to the Pass were exceedingly difficult, and the construction of a road would be very expensive and troublesome. There is a fine view of Chumalari from the Pass itself, but very little of the Phari Valley can be seen. The road by which we descended was a different one from that of the morning, and far worse. We crossed some considerable moraines, and in one place went over a Pass quite as difficult as the Yakla itself. At last a long and steep descent brought us into the Byutan Valley,

Visited the Yakla.

where my camp was pitched on the bank of a pretty stream, flowing through a wide flat covered with grass and rhododendron scrub.

Chomnaga and the Chola Pass.

Next day I crossed over to Chomnaga, or Chumanko, at the head of the beautiful fir-clad valley of the Dikchu, and encamped at about 12,300 feet, a little lower than the place where Doctors Hooker and Campbell were seized in 1849. On the way I went to visit some splendid pasture-lands, at the elevation of about 14,000 feet. On the following morning I went up to visit the Chola Pass. The ascent to this is much easier than that to the Yakla from Byutan; but it is much longer, steeper, and in every way more difficult, than that to the Jeylep, or even than that of the Gnatui; while even the Yakla would be in almost every way preferable as a trade route. At the Pass I met the Dewan, to whom I had written from the Yakla, asking him to meet me at Chomnaga, as several points on which I required information had occurred to me after he had left me at Jeylep. We spent a couple of days at Chomnaga discussing matters connected with Thibet, and I made the Dewan reduce to writing the answers which he gave to my questions. He left me on the 10th, and on the 11th I started for Tumlong.

Information about Thibet.

As during the rest of my tour I concerned myself more with the affairs of Sikhim than with Thibet, I may conveniently here throw together some information regarding the latter country which may be of interest.

Routes.

I shall not attempt to make much addition to what is known or conjectured of the geography of Thibet; for I believe that attempts to piece together descriptions of a country from the account of others are almost always worse than useless. I may mention, as an illustration of this, that the information received by me concerning the road from Phari to

Lassa differs very considerably from the itineraries of Klaproth, Dr. Campbell, and Major Lance, each of which differs from the other two. The route, however, between Phari and Giantzi, as described to me, coincides with that actually taken by Turner, both taking five days, while three out of the four intermediate halting-places are identical. Klaproth and Major Lance makes Giantzi to be the ninth stage from Phari, while according to Dr. Campbell it is the twelfth. From Giantzi to Nagarchi I make three stages, crossing the Kurula on the last day. Klaproth has four stages, Dr. Campbell eight. From Nagarchi to Lassa my information gives five days, Klaproth eight, and Dr. Campbell twenty-two. Major Lance has no place which I can identify with Nagarchi, and he makes ten stages between Giantzi and Lassa. The Sampoo, in the accounts received by me, is crossed on the second day after leaving Nagarchi. If my information is correct, Lassa is thirteen days from Phari, fifteen from Choombi, and sixteen from any of the Passes. Jigatzi is about two days from Giantzi. Turner arrived there on the morning of the third day.

I collected a considerable amount of information regarding the history and present political situation of Thibet. All that I heard on the latter subject supports the views which I submitted to Government in my report of the 13th of August last, and I shall only now give such leading facts as seem necessary for the proper understanding of the present report.

Early History of Bhuddism in Thibet.

Bhuddism is said to have been introduced into Thibet before the middle of the seventh century after Christ, and there is still in existence at Lassa a monastery founded about A.D. 650, according to the Thibetan chronologists. The sect now dominant in Thibet assert that

the form of Bhuddism which prevailed at first
was based on the purest teachings of Sakkia
Munni; but that about the middle of the following century Thibet was visited by Urgyen, or
Goor Rimbochay, an avatar who had miracu-
lously reappeared in India after an absence
from earth of some 1,600 years. It is alleged
that his teaching had a tendency to relax the
obligation of priestly celibacy, and that he
introduced many Brahminical symbols and
ritualistic observances. Goor Rimbochay, on
his way back to India, is said to have passed
through Sikhim, and to have chosen Tassiding
as the site of a monastery, which however was
not built till more than seven hundred years
later. For nearly two hundred years after
his departure, the modifications of the early
faith introduced by him were accepted without
question by all Bhuddists in Thibet; but in
the beginning of the eleventh century from
our era, Attisha, a native of Bengal, with his
disciple Bromston (pronounced Domton), pro-
tested against the Brahminical practices introduced by Goor Rimbochay, and against the low
estimate of the spiritual importance of celibacy
that marked his teaching. The followers of
Attisha, like the European reformers of the
sixteenth century, affected to believe that
whatever they disapproved of in the doctrine
or practice of the contemporaneous church was
a departure from primitive purity, and they
rejected everything except what appeared to
them to be contained in the teachings of
Sakkia Munni.

Out of this movement arose the great schism
in the Thibetan church. The reformers adopted
as their distinctive badge a yellow head-
dress, both in every-day life and in their religious ceremonials. They are called by several
names, of which the best known is that of

Gellookpa, which is really the name of a great sub-division of the sect which took its rise about the middle of the fifteenth century of our era. The followers of Goor Rimbochay, called Urgyenpa after him, are also styled Nyingmapa (the old sect); but probably the names by which the sect is best known to us are Brukpa (pronounced Dookpa) and Shammar. They adopted a red cap as their badge. The contests between these two great parties in the church lasted for several hundred years, and it is said that an appeal to arms was made more than once. For many years the adherents of the old faith seem to have had success on their side; but eventually the Gellookpa doctrines spread throughout all the Tartar tribes of Central Asia, and seem to have obtained a marked advantage in Thibet itself during the first half of the fifteenth century, mainly through the influence of two great teachers, one of whom founded the Genden monastery, near Lassa, which has ever since been one of the most famous seats of Bhuddist learning. The other, who founded the monastery of Bkrashis Lhunpo (pronounced Teshoo Loombo), near Jigatzi, it is said, on the ruins of a great Dookpa establishment, was the first Lama to whom the title of Rgyalva Rin-po-chhe (pronounced Gyow Rimbochay) was given, and he may be considered as the founder of the succession of priest-kings known to Europeans and the Chinese as Dalai Lamas. He died in the year 1473, according to a Thibet chronology obtained by Csoma de Koros. The successors of this Lama seem to have made use of their influence over the tribes of Central Asia to strengthen their position in Thibet; and in 1640, the fifth Dalai Lama made himself master of the entire country, with the assistance of a Mongol prince, according to Csoma de Koros; but this is not confirmed by my authorities.

Rise of the Dalai Lamas.

Spread of the Dookpa faith south of Thibet.

Meantime the adherents of the Dookpa sect, although reduced to submission, seem to have been allowed the free exercise of their religion, and they are still numerous in Thibet, where they retain many of their ancient seats, among others the great Sakkia monastery, celebrated for its library. There was, however, during the sixteenth and early part of the seventeenth centuries a steady flow of the more earnest members of the sect towards the regions now known as Bhootan, Sikhim, and East Nepal, where the Dookpa form of Bhuddism has prevailed to the present day. It is probable that at the outset the Dhurma Rajahs of Bhootan actually exercised some kind of supremacy over the churches established in all these regions. I have not been able to obtain exact information on this head; but it is certain that he has long claimed the headship of the whole sect. For instance, the legend on his seal, of which Dr. Hooker gives a transcript and translation, asserts that he is above all the Lamas of the Dookpa creed.

Relations between Thibet and China.

The fifth Dalai Lama, who, as mentioned above, became undisputed master of all Thibet, built the great monastic palace of Pota La, near Lassa, of which there is an interesting notice in Huc's work. He is said to have delegated the government of the province of Chang to the avatari Lama of Teshoo Loombo, who was called thenceforth Changpenchin Rimbochay, but who is best known to us as Teshoo Lama. This Dalai Lama entered into very close relations with the Mantchoo conquerors of China, and paid a visit to the Emperor Shunche, who is said to have received him with great honor, and to have enrolled himself among his disciples. It is probable, however, that even then the Chinese statesmen had initiated the policy, which has up to the present day been steadily adhered to, of attempting to neutralize

the enormous influence which the Dalai Lama
could exercise over the Tartar subjects of the
empire, by weakening his position in Thibet
and making him a dependant on the Emperor's
protection. Csoma de Koros says that the death
of this Dalai Lama was concealed for twelve
(according to one account, for eighteen) years
by a regent or Desi named Sangye. It is
possible that the origin of the curious office of
Noumehen, or Geshub Rimbochay, may have
been somehow connected with this affair; but
this is merely a conjecture; for I have not been
able to get any information about the beginning of the office or its early history. All that
I could learn was that, from time immemorial,
the oldest among the occupants of the four chairs
of the Chemeling, Tengiling, Chechooling, and
Kendooling monasteries, had the title of Geshub
Rimbochay, or image of the Gyow, was regent
during the Dalai Lama's minority, and, for
many years previous to 1844, practically the
temporal ruler of the country. These four
Lamas were avatari like the Dalai himself,
and seem to have been the natural leaders
of the party in Thibet opposed to Chinese
aggression.

The common historical handbooks state that
Thibet was completely conquered by China in
1720. I do not know what ground there is for
this assertion, except, perhaps, that about that
time the position and influence of the Chinese
representatives at Lassa, called Ampahs, may
have become greater and more defined than
before. Some time previous to that date,
the authority of the Dalai Lama over the
Bhuddist tribes of Central Asia had been used
by the Emperor Kang-He in putting down
a formidable religious rising, headed by
the great Lama of a monastery in the north of
Tartary, an interesting account of which is

given by the Abbé Huc; but this great service did not lessen the jealousy felt by the Imperial Government of the power of the Dalai Lama. For rather more than a century after this, Chinese policy in Thibet seems to have been mainly directed to lessen his spiritual influence by raising up a rival in the Teshoo Lama, whose reputation for sanctity was exalted by all means possible, and to embarrass the Government at Lassa by fostering the jealousy which the Teshoo Lama, as ruler of Chang under the Dalai Lama, felt at the encroachments of the Geshub Rimbochay, whom he looked upon as merely the regent of the eastern province of U, but who claimed to exercise the delegated power of the Dalai Lama throughout Thibet.

Massacre of Chinese in 1770.

In 1770 a Geshub was murdered in the house occupied by the Ampahs at Lassa, and his death was avenged by a general massacre of all the Chinese in Thibet. A war ensued, in which the Chinese, according to some accounts, were not very successful in the field; but were able, chiefly through the influence of the Teshoo Lama, to get the Thibetans to accept their terms. The Teshoo Lama seems to have been nominated Geshub Rimbochay by the Chinese Emperor as a reward for his services; but the Thibetans do not acknowledge him as a lawful regent, and there seems to have been a rival Geshub at Lassa.

Missions of Bogle and Turner, and attack of the Nepalese.

The Teshoo Lama, however, as regent, addressed Warren Hastings on behalf of the Bhooteas, with whom we were at war about the end of 1773. The Governor-General took advantage of this opening to send a mission to Teshoo Loombo. Mr. Bogle, who was selected for this mission, spent six months with the Teshoo Lama, who seems to have been really desirous of cultivating friendly relations with our Government, but who died in 1779 of smallpox in China, whither he had gone, according to Thibetan tradition, to solicit the active assistance of the Emperor against the rival Geshub at Lassa. His death made the latter ruler of Thibet for the time being, and Captain Turner, who was sent on a second mission to Teshoo Loombo in 1783, was obliged to return without having gained any definite advantage, owing, as his narrative clearly shows, to the opposition of the Geshub Rimbochay at Lassa. In 1790 the Nepalese invaded Thibet, plundered Teshoo Loombo, and returned to their own country with much booty. Captain Turner says that our Government declined to help the Thibetans in the matter; but I doubt whether its aid was asked for. However this may be, an appeal made to the Chinese Government was promptly responded to by the despatch of an army, which reduced the Nepalese to submission and exacted from them full reparation for the losses suffered by Thibet. The Imperial Government, however, took advantage of the opportunity to post Chinese troops at several points on the frontier of Nepal, Sikhim, and Bhootan, and to prevent the Thibet Government from re-establishing the trade between British India and the provinces of Chang which had existed previous to the Nepalese invasion.

The fifty years that followed was chiefly marked by Chinese encroachments, resisted often with success by the Thibetan national party, led by the Geshub for the time being. The Teshoo Lama, of whose marvellous precocity when aged eighteen months Turner gives a rather incredible account, seems to have grown up to be a man of uncommon ability and force of character, to which were joined the jealousy of the Geshub and the leaning towards China which had become

Revolution of 1843.

traditions of his office. A striking description of this Lama is given by the Abbé Huc, whose account of the events which took place in Lassa in 1843 has been corroborated in almost every particular by the information which 1 have received.

For many years previous to this time the Lama of Chemiling had been Geshub. He was an ambitious and imperious man, much disliked by the subordinates, though apparently not unpopular with the people generally, probably on account of his determined opposition to all encroachment on the part of the Ampahs. During his term of office two Dalai Lamas had died while minors, and when a third minor died in 1842-43, the enemies of the Geshub spread a report that the three Lamas had met with foul play at his hands. When the avatar of the Dalai Lama was again found, the Teshoo Lama, the two Ampahs, and the four Shaffees, or State Secretaries at Lassa, secretly signed and forwarded to China a document soliciting the Emperor to interfere to protect the child from the fate of his three predecessors. The Government of Pekin immediately despatched to Lassa a special commissioner with full powers to take any steps which he might think necessary in the matter. Keshen, who was chosen for the office, had been one of the eight Tong-Tongs, the highest functionaries of the empire, and had been sent in 1840 to Canton to conduct the war against England. But instead of fighting he concluded a treaty which was repudiated by the Emperor, and Keshen was condemned to death, a sentence which was afterwards commuted to imprisonment in chains in Mantchooria. He now received a conditional pardon and was sent to Lassa. On his arrival there he, with the aid of Shaffee and the Teshoo Lama, seized the chief adherents of the Geshub, and extracted from them, while under torture, statements implicating the Geshub. The latter, when he discovered the Tong-Tong's object, attempted a forcible resistance; but, after some show of fighting, he yielded and went off to China, as he asserted, to defend his cause before the Emperor.

After this the Tong-Tong and his supporters promulgated an edict of the Dalai Lama and the Emperor, declaring the four Lings for ever incapable of holding the office of Geshub, which, with some pretence of popular election, was bestowed on the Rating Lama, a young avatar of about eighteen. But the real ruler under the Tong-Tong was Shete Shaffee, an able and ambitious man, who probably had the chief hand in bringing about the revolution. He is the chief Kalon mentioned by the Abbé Huc, who formed a high opinion of his character and abilities. The Tong-Tong seems to have made great changes in the entire administration of Thibet, to have remodelled the whole of the civil offices, to have obtained for the Ampahs the complete control of frontier affairs, to have bound over the Thibet Government by very stringent agreements to the policy of isolation, and to have attempted the formation of something like a militia. After some time he was made Governor of Szechnen, and then contests arose between the Geshub Rating and Shete Shaffee, which ended in the former taking refuge in China and the latter assuming the office of Geshub. He resisted successfully the attack made by the Nepalese in, I think, 1855, and is said to have taken several guns from them.

On his death, the aged Lama of Genden, a man of great renown for learning and piety, became Geshub; and when he died, some months since, the Dalai Lama, who is a youth of about

Events since the fall of Chemeling.

eighteen, declared the office to be in abeyance, and undertook its duties in addition to his own spiritual functions. He is said to be much influenced by the advice of the Chechub Kembo, a great officer with somewhat anomalous functions, apparently partaking of those of Private Secretary and those of President of the Executive Board of Shaffees, or Secretaries, in whose hands is the administration of the province of U. The Teshoo Lama, who is at present on good terms with the Government of Lassa, is assisted in governing the province of Chang by a Shaffee and four Depens, of whom the Chechep Depen of Giantzi is the most important. All these officers are said to be appointed from Lassa, and though the Ampahs do not interfere formally in such appointments, their influence is said to be very great, and to be always exercised in the case of frontier posts.

Soon after the Dalai assumed the conduct of affairs, he got involved in a dispute between the Ampahs, which ended in the recall of one of them. The successor of the latter has, it is said, made up matters, and is on unusually friendly terms with the Dalai Lama, to whom he is represented to pay assiduous court. Since my return I have heard from the Sikhim Rajah that a special Commissioner of unusually high rank is reported to be on his way from Pekin to Lassa.

Military strength of Thibet.

I have been informed that the total strength of regular troops in the four garrisons of Lassa, Jigatzi, Giantzi, and Tingri, amounts at present to 3,800, of whom 2,300 are Thibetans and 1,500 are Chinese. Besides these there are said to be some Chinese soldiers stationed on the Military post road. The numbers given above are so much lower than I had expected, that I made many inquiries to satisfy myself of their correctness, but always with the same result. These troops are all armed with matchlocks. The Thibetans have a few old guns, which, as I understand, they took from the Nepalese in the last war, and several made on the same pattern which they have lately got from Batang, or perhaps Sifan. In addition to the regular force, there is a rudimentary system of militia, which is said to have been introduced by the Tong-Tong Kishen. The Governor of each fort has a small collection of weapons in his charge, and he is supposed to give a certain number of days' training in each year to all the young men able to carry arms within his jurisdiction; but the attendance seems to be almost voluntary, and I suspect that the system is almost ineffective.

I have not been able to collect any reliable statistics of the trade of Thibet, and any attempt on my part to estimate its extent would result in mere random guesses. The information I can give on this subject must therefore be very incomplete. *(Trade of Thibet.)*

The trade between Thibet and China is much less considerable than it had been often represented to be; and, owing to the badness and difficulty of the roads and the insecurity of much of the country through which they pass, I do not think there is much prospect of immediate increase. The chief articles exported by Thibet are ivory, rhinoceros-horns, peacocks' feathers, madder, and blankets,—the last of which probably do not go beyond the countries inhabited by the Tartar tribes. It is to be observed that all the above articles, except the blankets, are in the first instance imported by Thibet from India. *(With China.)*

There is reason to believe that opium is also obtained from Nepal and exported to

China in considerable quantities. I could get no local information on this head; but I conjecture from what I heard that the opium is abkarry. Inquiries are being made into the matter in Thibet, and I shall report the result when I hear it. Meantime I should suggest that inquiry be made in Nepal, through the Resident, and that vigilance be exercised in the frontier districts. Mr. Hodgson mentions that an illicit trade existed as early as 1831.

The imports from China are silks, an inferior description of woollen cloth, fine snuff, porcelain, and various other articles of luxury, the use of which must be confined to a very small class in a country like Thibet. But of course the chief article of import is tea, which is generally of a coarse description and unpleasant flavour. The price of this is eight annas the pound at Lassa. The Thibetans told me that they could not buy in Lassa tea as fine as some Darjeeling tea which I had with me, though as much as two rupees the pound is paid for the best tea procurable there. I have no doubt that if tea were freely admitted to Thibet, our Darjeeling growers could easily produce a tea of better quality than that now commonly consumed, and deliver it even at Lassa at a lower price than is now paid for the China article. But they would have to manufacture for the market, and break away from ideas formed under the influence of brokers catering for English tastes.

I doubt, however, whether there would ever be a large demand for the finer teas; but it is quite possible that a comparatively cheap supply might create a taste for such teas. The Phari Jungpen acknowledged to me that the prohibition of the importation of our tea is due to Chinese influence; and certainly a remonstrance on this head ought to be made by Her Majesty's representative at Pekin. At the same time I must point out that the policy followed by our growers has done much to make the exclusion possible. It is an almost incredible fact that Chinese tea is imported through Thibet into Darjeeling for the consumption of the native inhabitants of the district, who are practically unable to obtain the tea grown on the spot.

European goods are mainly imported into Thibet, through Nepal and Ladakh, by Cashmeree and Nepalese (Newar) traders who reside at the great marts. The imports by those routes are chiefly broadcloth, cottons of various kinds, pearls, coral, turquoise and some other precious stones, gold-embroidered stuffs, hookah tobacco, and opium. Of these articles, the most important is broadcloth, the demand for which in Thibet is very great. The woollen cloths manufactured in the country, though warm, are coarse and heavy, and those obtained from China are immeasurably inferior to broadcloth. As warm clothing is one of the first necessaries of life in Thibet, it will be easily understood that, practically for some time to come, the only limit to the demand for broadcloth in Thibet will be the want of means of purchasing it.

<small>Through Nepal and Ladakh.</small>

The chief exports from Thibet by the Nepal and Ladakh channels are blankets, musk, yaks' tails, borax, ponies, gold, and silver. The Cashmeree merchants are said to send gold and silver to India, in payment for the article imported by them, in preference to exporting any of the bulkier products of Thibet. Gold, the amount of which exported is comparatively insignificant, is almost always the produce of the country, and sent as bullion. I was told that the silver goes in the form of rupees, and that it has for the most part been imported from Assam by the Towang route, the Thibetans who trade on that frontier as a rule taking money in exchange for their goods.

And with Bhootan and Darjeeling.

The chief articles imported into Thibet from Bhootan and Darjeeling are rice, goor, and sugar; various sorts of dried fruits; tobacco, in leaf and for the hookah; stick lac, madder, indigo, red and white sandal-wood, ivory, rhinoceros-horns, peacocks' tails, and red and white endi cloth. The rice is mainly imported for the consumption of the Chinese in Thibet. The demand for indigo is very great, and the profit on it is greater than that on any other import, varying from fifty to one hundred per cent. on the cost of importing the article. This is accounted for by an alleged difficulty in getting it in small quantities from the producers, which creates a practical monopoly in favour of traders with, what is for Thibet, a large capital, while the use of the dye is universal in the country.

The exports to Bhootan and Darjeeling are tea, salt, blankets, silk piece-goods, ponies, mules, cows, sheep, yaks' tails, musk, turquoise, coral, and gold. The export of the three articles last named is very insignificant, and the demand is confined to Bhooteas. The fact that tea is imported into Bhootan and Darjeeling shows that there is something wrong in the policy pursued by our growers. The market for Thibet salt must for the present be almost exclusively local. It sells here for less than Rs. 8 the maund, while sea-borne salt fetches Rs. 10; that is nearly Rs. 6 more than the Calcutta price, and Rs. 4 more than the price at Purneah, the nearest intermediate station. When, however, there is a good road from one of the passes to a point on the North Bengal Railway, it may become a question whether we can allow the

Thibet salt to come in free of duty. It is
said that it does not pay to export blankets
of the best quality made in Thibet, where
they fetch higher prices than could be
obtained in Darjeeling. The coarse blankets
which do come in cost Rs. 1-8 or 2 each in
Thibet, and are sold here for Rs. 2 or 3.
I was also told that the current price for
good ponies in Thibet are higher than those
obtainable here, and that as a rule the ponies
exported are either of an inferior description
or very old. I believe this to be the case, for
I have remarked that almost all the good
ponies in the district are aged. I think that if
there were a good road, and if the dangerous
river Teesta were bridged, more valuable
ponies would be brought down.

But it is probable that such a road would do
far more to encourage the export to India of
cows and sheep, ghee and wool. Thibet, though
poor in every other respect, is really wealthy
in herds and flocks. No grazing-grounds that
I have seen or heard of in India can be compared with the splendid upland pastures of the
Chola range, with their rich lower slopes for a
winter refuge. The Thibetan cattle are good,
yielding comparatively large quantities of rich
milk, and making fair beef when killed at the
right time. Some of the breeds of sheep yield
a remarkably fine wool; and the mutton of
one kind, at least, when taken from its own
upland pastures, surpasses in flavour and delicacy anything I have tasted in India. Turner
considered this mutton to be the finest in
the world. Dr. Campbell speaks in very
high terms of all the Sikhim breeds of sheep.
At present these magnificent flocks and herds
are almost wasted for want of some means of
conveying them and their produce to the
markets of India. It is true that there is some

doubt whether the cows would live and give
milk in the plains, and it is certain that the
finest breed of sheep could not be kept alive
during the hot weather; but both cows and
sheep of all classes could be got even as far
as Calcutta in good condition during the cold
season, while sheep of the inferior breeds could
probably be got in safety to the districts near
the foot of the hills all through the rains.
There can be no doubt that very large quantities of wool, of which no use is at present
made, would be exported from Thibet and the
higher parts of Sikhim if there were an out-
let for it; and I think it probable that immense
quantities of ghee could be manufactured in
the pasturages, and sent down to the plains, at
a much lower cost than the present price of
ghee in most parts of Bengal. A bridge across
the Teesta, and a good road to the temperate
pastures, are all that are required to develop
to the utmost these branches of the Thibet
export trade; and until we have such road and
bridge, these splendid flocks and herds will
remain practically out of our reach, and of little
value to their owners, compared to what they
would be if their produce could be exchanged
for broadcloth and indigo, tea and tobacco.
I have therefore no hesitation in recommending
that no time be lost in bridging the Teesta, and
making a road through Sikhim to the Chola
range. I shall, lower down, consider at what
point it would be advisable to bridge the
Teesta, and what would be the best line for the
road to take.

VIEW OF CHOLA RANGE FROM ENCH. WITH MONKS IN THE FOREGROUND.

PART II.

SIKHIM PROPER.

VIEW OF RUMTIK MONASTERY, SHOWING ARRANGEMENT OF MONKS' HOUSES.

CAMP AT PEMIONGCHI.

SIKHIM PROPER.

OUR road from Chomnaga lay at first along the banks of the Dikchoo, which, for several miles from the foot of Chola, flows through a narrow valley of extraordinary beauty. On either side were lofty crags, most picturesque in form and rich in colour, while the valley itself was covered with many varieties of rhododendrons, and with silver firs, some of which were unusually fine. One of the rhododendrons bears poisonous leaves; and there is in the valley a herb, also poisonous, the name of which I do not know. Several of the sheep which I had received from the Sikhim people and the Jungpens were poisoned by one or other of these plants, the existence of which in the valley is a strong argument against making a trade road through it. After some miles of almost imperceptible descent, the index of the aneroid, which had stuck fast half-way between 20 and 31 since the 30th October, began to move up, and it had risen to one point short of 20 when we reached our camping-ground at a place called Towrang. Here I had to wait for a couple of days for fresh supplies for my coolies, which were following me all round the passes. I had thought it best to get these supplies from Darjeeling, in order to make my tour as little burdensome as I could to the people of Sikhim.

On the 14th I left Towrang. The path almost immediately leaves the valley and ascends the ridge to the north, becoming in

From Chomnaga to Kubbi.

many places steep and difficult. The aneroid very quickly fell to its lowest point, and the index ceased to move. After this we ascended some hundred feet, leaving the firs and the rhododendrons below us, until at last we reached the summit, covered with dwarf rhododendrons and bamboo. There is said to be a splendid view across Sikhim from this hill, which is called Pyung-gong; but when I crossed it everything was shrouded in dense fog. The descent from Pyung-gong is steep, rocky, and very bad, though, owing to its being on the main route between Toomlong and Choombi, there had been evidently much labour spent in attempts made from time to time to improve it. We passed rapidly through bamboo and scrub rhododendrons to firs and juniper, and then to oaks, the rhododendrons getting larger and more varied as we descended. On a great flat in the oak forest there were many black yaks'-hair tents of the Rajah's herdsmen, on their way from the upland pastures, with great herds of yaks, all of which were said to belong to the Rajah. Next day we still descended, but more gradually, and we occasionally came to comparatively level bits, and sometimes to slight ascents. After several hours' walking we got to a narrow ridge at about 5,300 feet, with the valley of the Dikchoo to the east and that of the Rutto to the west. At this point the road from west to east, leading from Toomlong to Guntuck, crosses the north and south road, along which we had come, leading from the Chola Pass to the Teesta, and thence to Darjeeling by a more direct route than that *viâ* Toomlong. I left this route and took the road to the right leading to Toomlong, and after a short descent halted at a place called Kubbi, from which we could see the Rajah's house and the Toomlong monasteries scattered over the face of the opposite ridge.

At Kubbi I got a note from Major Judge, R.E., who had been good enough to consent to take Major Lindsay's place, and who had just arrived at Toomlong and wished to know what he was to do. I asked him to come over next day, when we settled that he should go off to Guntuck and explore the route from there to the Chola range, while I should go across to Toomlong and see the officials who had been left there to conduct affairs during the Rajah's absence, and then meet Major Judge at Guntuck on his return from the Chola range. He had brought with him a photographic apparatus, with some dry plates, which had been lent him by Mr. Phillips, of Darjeeling; and a larger lens, which Messrs. Doyle and Company had lent to Major Lindsay, but which had been delayed on the road, now came up. Major Judge took both instruments with him, and attempted to photograph several views on the range. After his return we both took pictures, but were not very successful.

Kubbi to Toomlong.

On the 17th Major Judge left for Guntuck, and I went across to Toomlong, passing through the Kubbi village cultivation. The people of this village pay their chief revenue to Thibet, but are bound to do certain services for the Sikhim Rajah, and to supply some food for his household. In explanation of this, I was told that the people were really Thibetans, and that though they happened to live at present in the territory of the Sikhim Rajah, and to cultivate land there, this did not release them from their obligations to their own State. They cultivate rice, murwa, maize, and buck-wheat. I did not see much wheat or barley till we got near the Teesta. Cardamoms and oil-seeds are mainly cultivated in the low valleys in the extreme west of Sikhim.

In a fallow field near the road, I passed the encampment of a trader returning from Thibet, where he had gone four months previously with his wife and children. He was a native of Toomlong, who had borrowed Rs. 400 at the Darjeeling bazaar at the rate of 24 per cent. per annum. He had invested the money in broadcloth, which he had exchanged in Thibet for a pony and 250 sheep. He expected to get Rs. 50 for the pony and an average of Rs. 3 each for as many of the sheep as might reach Darjeeling alive; but he expected to lose at least 10 or 12 in crossing the Teesta and in the hot, steamy valleys of that river and the Rungeet, while if he were unlucky he might lose fifty or sixty.

After leaving Kubbi, we descended into the deep tropical valley of the Rutto, the heat of which seemed intense after the cold of the Chola range. The valley, however, was exquisitely beautiful. The road went along the bank of the stream for some way to its junction with the Ryott, a small stream which drains the Toomlong hill. After going up the stream a little, we crossed it and ascended rapidly to Toomlong, where I found a tent of the Rajah's pitched for me near his own house, the exterior of which has been described by Hooker.

Stay at Toomlong.

The greater part of the interior is occupied by two chapels,—one on the ground floor and one above. In the latter of these a very curious function was being celebrated while I was at Toomlong. It was part of the funeral rites of the Rajah's sister, who had died a few days after his return to Choombi from the Jeylep Pass. The body of the dead woman had, I believe, been buried at Choombi; but her clothes and other property had been sent to her mother's house at Toomlong, where a lay-figure meant

THE RAJAH'S HOUSE AT TOOMLONG.

to represent her, dressed in her costume as a nun, and wearing a gilt mitre and a long white veil, was placed on a kind of throne to the right of the great altar in the principal chapel.

Before the figure was a table, on which were different kinds of food; on another table at the side were various things which had belonged to the woman when alive; while on a third, 108 little brass lamps were arranged in rows. Long lines of monks, in dark red robes and with very tall caps of bright crimson on their heads, sat on carpets placed in the middle of the chapel and chanted litanies throughout each day of my stay at Toomlong.

It chanced that I saw the conclusion, and learned the meaning of this ceremony at Pemiongchi, where the lay-figure of the nun was taken some days after I left Toomlong. There for three days the figure was seated before the altar, and the monks chanted the litanies for the departure of the soul of the dead nun which had accompanied her clothes from Choombi. On the third day the relations, friends, and dependents of the deceased brought or sent gifts of food, or clothing, or money, which were all laid before the figure of the dead woman; while the head Lama, standing in front of his chair and turning towards the figure, stated the nature of each gift and the name of the donor. Towards evening the tea-cup of the nun was freshly filled with tea and her murwa jug with murwa, and all the monks solemnly drank tea with her. Then many people who had known and loved the nun when alive, went up, and, prostrating themselves before the figure, kissed the hem of the robe as a last farewell; while the monks chanted the litanies more zealously than ever, and the head Lama, who had left his chair and gone to one of the tables, went through some elaborate ceremonies

Funeral ceremonies at Pemiongchi.

the meaning of which I could not make out.
At about nine o'clock the chanting ceased,
and the Lama, again standing in front of his
chair, made a long speech to the soul of the
nun, in which he told her that all that could
be done to make her journey to another world
easy had been done, and that now she would
have to go forth alone and unassisted to appear
before the King and Judge of the dead:—" You
will have to leave your robes, your mitre, and
your veil," said he, "and you will be shown in
the mirror of the just king, clad in the black
garment of your sins, or in the shining garment of your good deeds. Your gold and
silver, your rank, your dependents, your good
name in this world will not help you now,
when your good deeds will be weighed in the
scales of the King against your evil deeds.
If you have done ill you will be punished; but
if your sins are found to be lighter than your
good works, your reward will be great indeed."
When the Lama had finished his address, some
of the monks took down the lay-figure and
undressed it; while others formed a procession
and conducted the soul of the nun into the
darkness outside the monastery, with a discordant noise of conch-shells, thigh-bone
trumpets, Thibetan flutes, gongs, cymbals,
tambourines, drums, and other most disagreeable but nameless instruments. I have described this ceremony at some length, as I have
not seen it noticed elsewhere; while it is an
interesting illustration of the church in Sikhim
in one of its most curious aspects.

The profit of this ceremony to the dead.

It is evidently one of the most important
functions of the Sikhim monks to help the soul
of the dead to make the journey from this
world to the abode of the terrible king of death,
who holds a mirror in which the naked soul is
reflected; while an attendant demon holds the

scales in which good deeds, poured in by the guardian Lama of the deceased, are weighed, against the evil deeds collected by a demon—probably his evil genius. If the verdict of the mirror and the scales be favorable, the Lama conducts the soul to abodes of bliss, where it apparently sings hymns and plays a kind of lute for an indefinite period; but if the mirror and the scales show more bad deeds than good, the soul is handed over to the tormentors,—most mediæval-looking demons, who inflict tortures of a varied character, but generally having some reference to the sins of the offender.

Ceremonies of the kind above described are considered absolutely necessary to the welfare of the dead, but they must be a most cruel tax on the living; for the Sikhim monks—an immensely big fraction of the whole population—are mainly supported on the profits derived from them.

Its cost to the living.

The right of conducting the souls of the inhabitants of each village to another world belongs to a particular monastery, and it would be contrary to etiquette—perhaps unlawful—for the monks of any other monastery to interfere in the matter. Sometimes one monastery burns the body of a deceased person, while another takes charge of the departing soul. In this case both monasteries are entitled to dues. The amount expended on these occasions is sometimes enormous, in proportion to the means of the people; but there is a universal custom which somewhat lessens the burden. When a member of a family dies, all the relations, friends, and dependents, send presents to the survivors, as a help to the deceased on the journey to the other world; and of course all these offerings go to the Lamas.

There are three monasteries near Toomlong —viz., Labrong, Pheydong, and Phonchong, which, in addition to the income derived from funeral ceremonies, from the offerings of the faithful, and from the sale of consecrated medicines, hold grants of land free of revenue, while the monks are exempted from all State burthens. The most important of these monasteries is Labrong, the head of which is really the superior of Pemiongchi, and of nearly two-thirds of the monasteries of Sikhim. He is called the Kupgain Lama, and is the avatar of the founder of Pemiongchi, which monastery was the residence of all his predecessors until some years ago, when the avatar appeared in the family of the last Rajah, whose eldest son, the brother of the present Rajah, was discovered to be Kupgain. The Rajah, in order to have his son near him, founded the Labrong monastery for him, where he resided till, on the death of his second brother, who had been held to be heir to Sikhim, a dispensation was obtained for his marriage, and he was acknowledged to be heir-apparent. He died, however, without children, and his next surviving brother, the present Rajah, was taken from the Phodong monastery, of which he was Lama, married, and declared heir-apparent. The avatar of the Kupgain Lama re-appeared in a very humble family. He is a young man, seemed rather stupid, and his manner was awkward.

Besides the Rajah's dwelling and the monasteries, there are scattered over the Toomlong hill a number of substantial-looking houses, belonging to various officials. Each house is surrounded by some cultivated land, in which are generally a few clumps of bamboos or fruit-trees. Many of these houses were unoccupied at the time of my visit, their owners being absent at Choombi. But I saw two officers who were styled Dewans, and who had been left at Toomlong in charge of the affairs there. They were represented as being very unfriendly to

HOUSES AT TOOMLONG.

GUNTUCK KAZI'S HOUSE.

Changzed, but they did not let this appear in conversation with me.

On the 21st I returned to Kubbi, and on the same day went on to a village named Chetok, to the east of the Dikchoo. We crossed that river at an elevation of less than 3,000 feet, though I do not think that the distance from the point where I had left it, at more than 11,000 feet, could have been as much as five miles in a straight line. Next day I went on to Guntuck, passing through some very well-cultivated land at first and then through dense forest, after which we came on the broad and richly-cultivated slopes of Ench, which adjoin those of Guntuck, and are in the jurisdiction of a nephew of the Kazi of the latter place. My camp was pitched on the ridge between the houses of the Kazis of Guntuck and Ench; and a few hundred feet higher up the ridge towards the north was a small monastery built and supported by the Guntuck family. Towards the south the ridge became very wide, and there was much level land on it. In one place were heaps of building materials and the foundations of a house begun by the Rajah's father. But the work was interrupted by his death, and has not been since resumed, though, as before mentioned, the idea of removing the residence of the Rajah to this place from Toomlong has not been abandoned. Below this is the house of the Kazi of Guntuck, a very unornamental building, of wattle and daub, raised on stout posts.

The slopes of the hill on either side are very gentle, and there is much ground suitable for buildings situated at elevations varying between 5,000 and 6,000 feet. There are six springs of water near the top of the ridge. On the whole, the place itself would be suited for a mart; but it is more than

Visit to Guntuck.

questionable whether the best route from Darjeeling to the Chola range lies through it. I have been only over that portion of the route which lies between the Teesta and Guntuck; but Major Judge, who went carefully over the whole distance, has given me a note on the subject, which I append to this report, and which I think will be found to be of much value.

Sikhim revenue system.

The Guntuck Kazi is one of the most influential officials in Sikhim, and there are more than eight hundred homesteads on the lands which are under his charge. There are twelve Kazis in Sikhim, and several other officers of various names exercise jurisdiction over specific tracts of lands. Each of these officers assesses the revenue payable by all the people settled on the lands within his jurisdiction, and, as far as I can make out, keeps the greater portion for himself, paying over to the Rajah a certain fixed contribution. At the same time, he has no proprietary right in the lands, though the Kazis have at least a kind of hereditary title to their office. The Kazis and other officers exercise limited civil and criminal jurisdiction within the lands the revenue of which they collect, all important cases being referred to the Rajah and decided by Changzed and the Dewans, who are at present three in number.

The cultivators have no title to the soil, and a man may settle down on and cultivate any land he may find unoccupied without going through any formality whatever, and when once he has occupied the land, no one but the Rajah can turn him out. But the Rajah can eject him at any time; and if he should cease to occupy the land, he would not retain any lien upon it. There is a kind of tenant-right, however, under which cultivators are enabled to dispose of unexhausted improvements. Thus, as it was explained to me, a man who has terraced a piece of hill-side could not sell the land, but is allowed to sell the right of using the terraces. This custom is acknowledged not to be absolutely a right, but more of the nature of an indulgence on the part of the Rajah, by whom it was allowed to grow up for the sake of convenience.

The land is not assessed, and pays no revenue. The assessment is on the revenue-payer personally, and I think that in theory he is supposed to be allowed the use of the Rajah's land in order that he may live and be able to render to the Rajah the services which he is bound to do as the Rajah's live chattel; and possibly if the system were carried to theoretical perfection, he would be bound to give over to the Rajah all the produce of the land—that is, all the fruit of his labour beyond what might be actually necessary to support himself and his family (a). In practice the subject is only bound to give a certain portion of his labour, or of the fruit of his labour, to the State; and when he does not give actual service, the amount of his property is roughly assessed, and his contribution to the State fixed accordingly; but such assessment is made without the slightest reference to the amount of land occupied by the subject. The value of his wives and children, slaves, cattle, furniture,

---

(a).—Among some of the ruder tribes on the North-East Frontier, there seems to have been absolutely no true conception of private property until the idea was learned from contact with Bengali traders. Previously everything belonged to the Chief, and no one ever imagined that a private individual had any proprietary right in any of his acquisitions as against the Chief. Of course the latter, as a general rule, allowed the subjects to retain possession of as much of what they acquired as he did not immediately want, but it was by way of loan. In the same way even now the Chief frequently permits favorites or members of his household to make use of articles of value which he had appropriated for himself, or which had been given to him personally by our Government. This has sometimes given rise to the supposition that a tribal community of goods existed among these races; but the truth lies in exactly the opposite direction. The tribe, its lands, and all that it possessed, belonged absolutely to the Chief.

&c., are all taken into account, but not the extent of his fields.

I believe this to be the revenue system in all Indo-Chinese States. It is so in Munnipore, Bhootan, Thibet, Sikhim, and, I believe, in Burmah. It was so in Cachar and Assam, and indeed the Assam land revenue system bears traces of it to this day. I have been told that in Nepal Sir Jung Bahadoor is trying hard to substitute for it a system based on some sort of ownership in and liability to pay according to the land actually held. I believe that a system something like that which I have tried to describe above is indicated in the 47th Chapter of Genesis; and it is interesting to remark, that just as in Egypt the land of the priests "became not Pharoah's," so in Sikhim the Lamas are not bound to labour for the Rajah, and pay no dues of any kind, no matter how much land may be cultivated by themselves or their bondsmen. It is possible that the forced labour and Vice-regal monopolies, of which we hear so much in modern Egypt, may have underlying them the theory that the chief of the State is absolute owner of all its subjects, as well as of all its land; and I have conjectured, in reading books about China, that such a theory may enter into some at least of the land-revenue systems of that empire.

Guntuck to the Teesta.

Major Judge returned from the Bhootan range on the 23rd, and we spent the 24th and 25th in exploring the ground round Guntuck, and in not very successful attempts to take photographs. On the 26th we left for the Teesta and the country to the west of it. We took different routes on the first day, Major Judge making a detour in order to explore a route by which I thought a considerable amount of ascent and descent might be avoided. This, however, turned out not to be the case. The road taken by me led down by an easy descent to a pretty stream called the Rumjun, crossed by a very ricketty bridge. From the stream I went up by a considerably longer and steeper ascent to the monastery of Rumtik, where we encamped. The church of the monastery was small, and rather poor-looking, but there are said to be eighty monks attached to it—a larger number than there are at any of the Sikhim monasteries, except Pemiongchi and Ralong. This is due to the great reputation of the head Lama, who comes from the Chinese frontier of Thibet. The monks' houses were very neat and well built, arranged in rows near the chapel. I tried to take two or three photographs of this monastery, as it is a very good example of the way in which the houses of the monks are generally grouped round a monastic church; but Mr. Doyle was not able to develop any of these plates, except one.

Next day our road was very uneven, and we had to make several steep though short ascents and descents; but the country through which we passed was exceedingly beautiful. After leaving Rumtik, we ascended to the top of the ridge and then descended a very steep and bad road to a series of wide, flat valleys, admirably cultivated, with pretty villages half hidden by groves of bamboos, plantains, and dark green orange-trees laden with ripe golden fruit. After going up and down among these for some miles, we descended considerably to a stream ; after crossing which we went up the easy slope of a wide hill covered with well-tilled farms and homesteads, standing in fields of young wheat or barley, which were surrounded by well-made fences, and dotted with orange-trees or picturesque clumps of bamboos and plantains, reminding one of the scenery in pictures of Chinese country life. Our camp was pitched on the ridge of this hill, at a place called Sang, where there is a very fine example of the religious structures called mendongs. These are thick walls of stones, sometimes of enormous length, ornamented with slabs inscribed with the sacred formula, "Om Mani Padmi Om," and having frequently recesses for burning juniper-wood, which are surmounted by little cupolas or towers to act as chimneys. The chait is another religious object frequently met in Sikhim. It is generally built in memory of the dead.

The Teesta to Lingdon.

On the 27th we descended by a road, in some places very steep, to the Teesta, which we crossed at an elevation of 1,575 feet. There was a cane bridge over the river, and my ponies were ferried across in a raft, on which I also crossed. The raft was made of bamboos, and was of precisely the same V-like form as those which the Lushais make to carry their salt up the Sonai, and as those which are used to cross some of the rivers on the Munnipore road. The river is very wide and rapid here, and the crossing is nearly as dangerous as that below the junction of it with the Rungeet, on the road to Kalimpoong. After crossing we went along for some way through a dense, foul-smelling forest, very suggestive of fever and ague, and then came upon the road from Darjeeling to Toomlong, at some point on Major Judge's route from Lingmo to Tingtee, described in his note under the date of November 14th. After going along this path, which was a very good one, for some time, we encamped on a comparatively open piece of ground near the junction of a large stream, called the Rungpo, with the Teesta. Near us were the huts of some herdsmen, who had made the clearance and who had brought down their cattle for winter pasture, the grazing on

GROUP OF CHAITS.

p. 66.

the lower slopes of the hills above the Teesta being very good.

Next day we left the Teesta Valley, and ascended a very steep path leading up a spur of Mainom, a great hill more than 11,000 feet high on the same range as Tendong. Upon this spur, at about 5,300 feet, is situated the Yangong monastery, where we pitched our camp. The view from the monastery is very striking. The valley of the Teesta, with the river winding like a silver thread through tropical forests, is clearly visible 4,000 feet below; while the zones of vegetation on the side of Mainom, from the screw-pines and fig-trees on the banks of the Teesta to the silver firs on the top, can be clearly distinguished with a good glass. Below Yangong is a pretty little lake, the genius of which is supposed to be the wife of the genius of the Mainom mountain. All great mountains, according to Lepcha mythology, are wedded to lakes. Thus Catsuperri is the wife of Kinchingunga, and Cholomo is the wife of Donkiah. The church of the Yangong monastery was being built when Dr. Hooker visited the place, which he calls Neongong, in 1848. It is one of the largest and best built of all those that I have seen in Sikhim, but it does not seem to have been finished. The inside walls are bare, and there are scarcely any appliances of worship. There is, however, a richly-ornamented doorway, something like one at Pemiongchi. But I think the door-way at Yangong was much handsomer, and indeed the finest thing of the kind which I saw in Sikhim. I tried to get a photograph of it, but unluckily the plates developed nothing.

From Yangong we crossed the ridge connecting Tendong with Mainom, at 6,824 feet. On our way up we passed the rock called

"Domani," or "Stone of Prayer," which is described by Dr. Hooker. From the ridge we descended to 5,349 feet, where we halted on ground formerly occupied by a village named Lingdam, which has now been removed to another site in the neighbourhood. The road from Yangong to Lingdam lies for the most part through a fine forest of oak and chestnut.

The Tassiding monastery was on a hill opposite to Lingdam, and appeared quite near; but the great Rungeet was between, the bridge over which was under repair, and I had to halt at Lingdam for a day till it was ready. While there I received a visit from one of the two great Lamas of Pemiongchi, who was on his way, with some of his monks, to meet Changzed and the Chota Rajah at Toomlong. He had with him the young son of Cheeboo Lama, who is joint owner with his cousin, one of the Sikhim Dewans, of the vast estate of more than one hundred square miles, which our Government gave to his father in the belief that it contained something like four thousand acres. The boy is being educated at Pemiongchi, and I am very anxious to get him into Darjeeling to have him taught English and to get him away from the Sikhim people, who I suspect want to make a Lama of him. I have arranged that he is to come in as soon as our proposed school gets properly established, and I think that the monks have given up for the present the idea of turning him into a Lama.

Tassiding

Next day we went to Tassiding, where we halted for a day close to one of the chapels, which are three in number, surrounded by groups of chaits. One of the three chapels belongs to the monastery of Pemiongchi, and is served by a monk deputed from there. This was in much better repair than the other

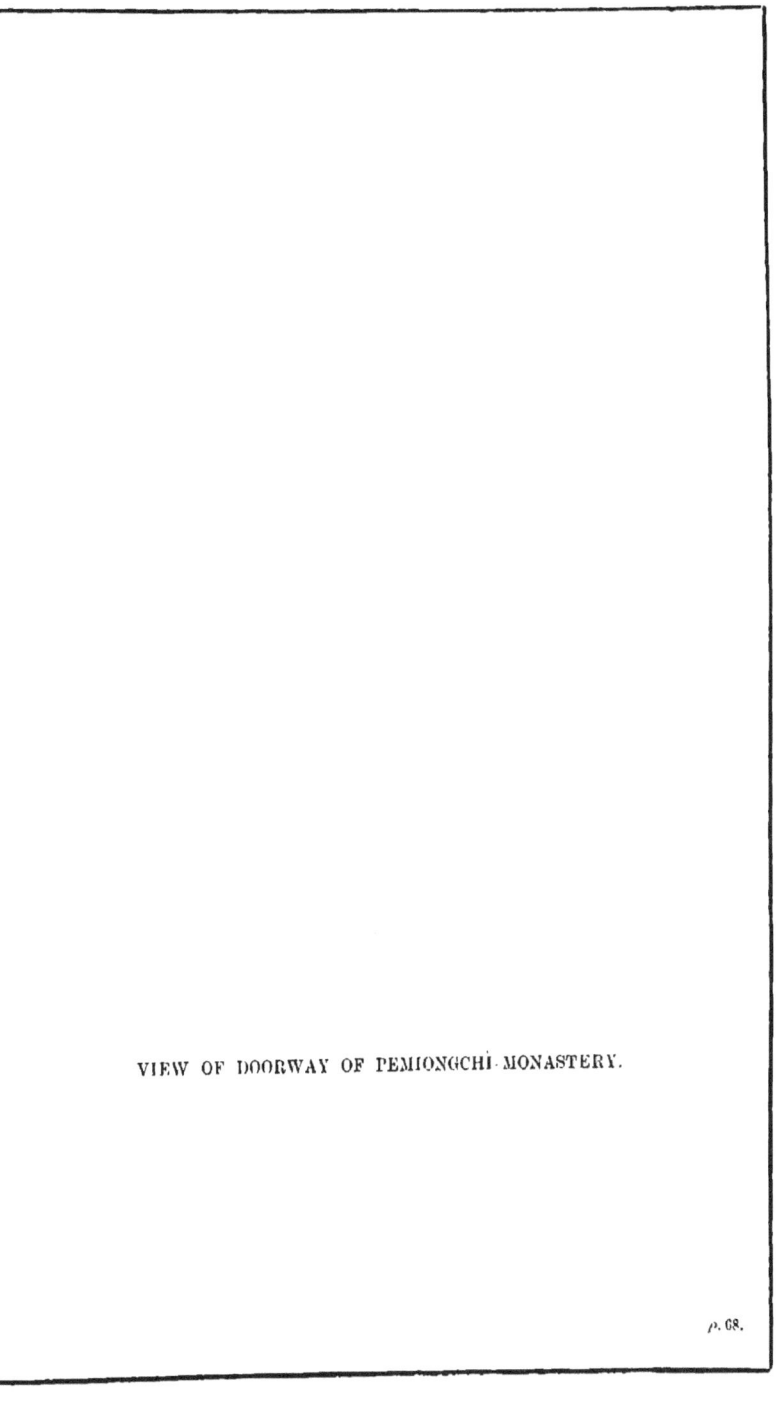

VIEW OF DOORWAY OF PEMIONGCHI MONASTERY.

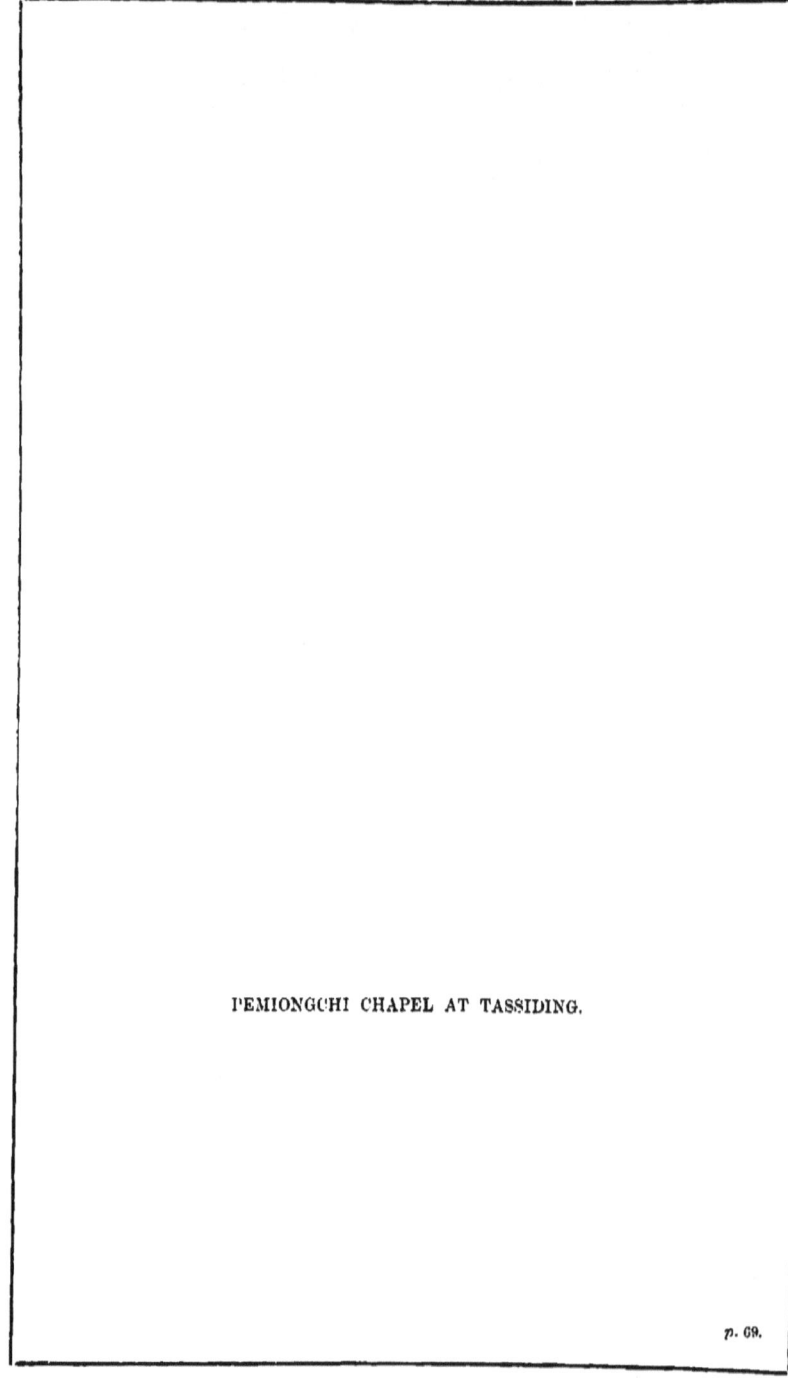

PEMIONGCHI CHAPEL AT TASSIDING.

two chapels, which had a poverty-stricken and uncared-for look about them, which contrasted strongly with the appearance of some of the younger and less noted monasteries. The monk-houses, too, were much in want of repair, and some of them were in ruins and unoccupied.

The present decayed state of this monastery, the most ancient and even still the most venerated in Sikhim, was attributed to the fact that its lawful head lives in Thibet. Probably, too, the claim of the Deb Rajah to interfere in support of a claimant to the Lama's chair of the monastery has had something to do with its decay. I have alluded in a previous part of this report to the evident unwillingness of the Sikhim durbar to discuss this subject, or to acknowledge that the Deb Rajah had made any pretence of exercising a right when he interfered in favour of the alleged avatar. I suspected, however, that the Deb Rajah had not interfered without a pretext; that the pretext was that the Bhootan church possessed some kind of supremacy over that of Sikhim; and that the Sikhim durbar concealed this through a natural wish to avoid the appearance of referring such a question to our Government for decision. I had therefore resolved to visit Tassiding and Pemiongchi with a view to making inquiries there. I was informed by the monks that more than three hundred years ago, three professors of the Dookpa faith, discontented with the pre-eminence of the Gelookpas in Thibet, left their respective monasteries, and, after many wanderings to and fro, all met at Yaksun under Kunchinjinga. Here, by a chance which they looked on as providential, they were found by the ancestor of the Rajahs of Sikhim, Pencho Namgay, then residing at Guntuck, apparently as a private person. The result of the meeting was an agreement that the three

Tradition about the foundation of the Sikhim State.

Lamas should attempt to convert the Lepchas and form a church among them, and that they should endeavour to make Pencho Namgay Rajah of the whole country. They succeeded in both attempts. The new Rajah removed his residence from Guntuck to Rabdenchi, hard by Pemiongchi, where there are still the picturesque ruins of a fort built by him. One of the Lamas founded a monastery near Dikkiling. Another, whose avatar is the Kupgain Lama, first settled at Changachelling; but afterwards removed his chair to Pemiongchi, on the same range of hills. The third built two of the Tassiding churches, on the site prophetically chosen by Goor Rimbochay seven hundred years before.

Claim to the chair of the Tassiding Lama.

This last Lama married and had children; consequently it is said his avatar has never re-appeared; but his successors have always been chosen from his family, which still exists and supplies monks to one of the greatest Dookpa foundations in Thibet. The present Lama fears the rains, pipsas, and leeches of Sikhim, and resides in the Thibetan monastery. Some years ago a rumour came from Bhootan that the avatar of Gnadeh, the Tassiding founder, had appeared in that country. A deputation of monks went to inquire into the matter, among whom were two of those with whom I talked. They came to the conclusion that the claim made on behalf of the Bhootea child was unfounded, and that Gnadeh still, as heretofore, remained without an avatar. But the child, when grown up, persisted in the claim made for him in his infancy, and has always asserted that he is the re-appeared Gnadeh.

Interference of Deb Rajah.

The Deb Rajah took up his claim some time since, and has written several letters on his behalf. I got a copy of one of these, which was addressed to the Pemiongchi Lamas, in

NORTH CHAPEL AT TASSIDING.

which the Deb Rajah says that the Bhootea claimant is the avatar of the great Tassiding Lama, and that if the Pemiongchi Lamas do not see that he gets his rights, it will not be well with them. The letter is rather rambling and inconsecutive; but the Deb appears to base his claims to interfere on the grounds that the Sikhim temples, and the images in them, were formerly repaired by the people of Bhootan, and that according to an old record Sikhim and Bhootan were under the same head at one time. The tone of the letter is very insolent. The Deb says that the Rajah of Sikhim is a fool, and that his officers do not perform their duties; but there are no explicit threats. I have heard, though, that in one letter, addressed to the Rajah himself, the Deb threatened to attack Sikhim, unless the avatar was placed in the chair at Tassiding.

It will be seen that this letter to the Pemiongchi people seems to point at some claim to the temporal rule of Sikhim founded on "the old record," but I do not think this is more than a flourish. On the other hand, I have no doubt that the Dhurma Rajah had once some kind of connection with the Sikhim church. There are many traces of this; for instance, one of the most prominent pictures on the walls of the North Chapel at Tassiding is a portrait of a Dhurma Rajah in his priestly robes. At the same time I do not think that we should recognize any claim on the part of the Bhootan Government to interfere in Sikhim monasteries, or even allow it to open the question; and I further think that we should use our influence to prevent the Deb Rajah writing insolent letters to the Rajah or his subjects.

There is not much to be said about the relations of Sikhim with the remaining two States on its borders. I was told that the

Relations of Sikhim with Nepal and Thibet.

Durbar has no relations nor communications with Nepal; but they evidently fear that State, and dislike the people. Sikhim is looked upon by Thibet as a dependent State. The Rajahs have always been in the habit of marrying Thibetan women, and for three generations their chief and favorite residence has been at Choombi. Up to a recent period they held large grants of land in Thibet,—or, to speak more correctly, the rights of the Thibetan State over these lands had been made over to them. But most of the grants have been resumed, and the Rajah now has jurisdiction over little more than the land around his house at Choombi. Although the Sikhim church still adheres to the distinctive doctrines of the Dookpa sect, and learned monks insist on the importance of the points in which they differ from the Gellookpas; still the plenary authority of the Dalai Lama is, with curious inconsistency, admitted, and knotty points connected with the internal administration of the church are said to be from time to time referred to him by the Rajah for decision.

Pemiongchi. From Tassiding we went to Pemiongchi, descending by a steep path to the Ratong, a very rapid stream, which comes down from the Kunchinjinga glaciers, and flows, at the place where we crossed it, through one of the most glorious tropical forests I have ever seen. From the Ratong the ascent to Pemiongchi is very long, but the road is a remarkably well-aligned one. It was made by the monks, and I doubt whether its gradient could be materially improved without increasing its length enormously.

Near the top I was met by drummers, fifers, and gong-beaters, who played a not unmusical march before me, till we arrived at the foot of the great platform on which the chapel is built.

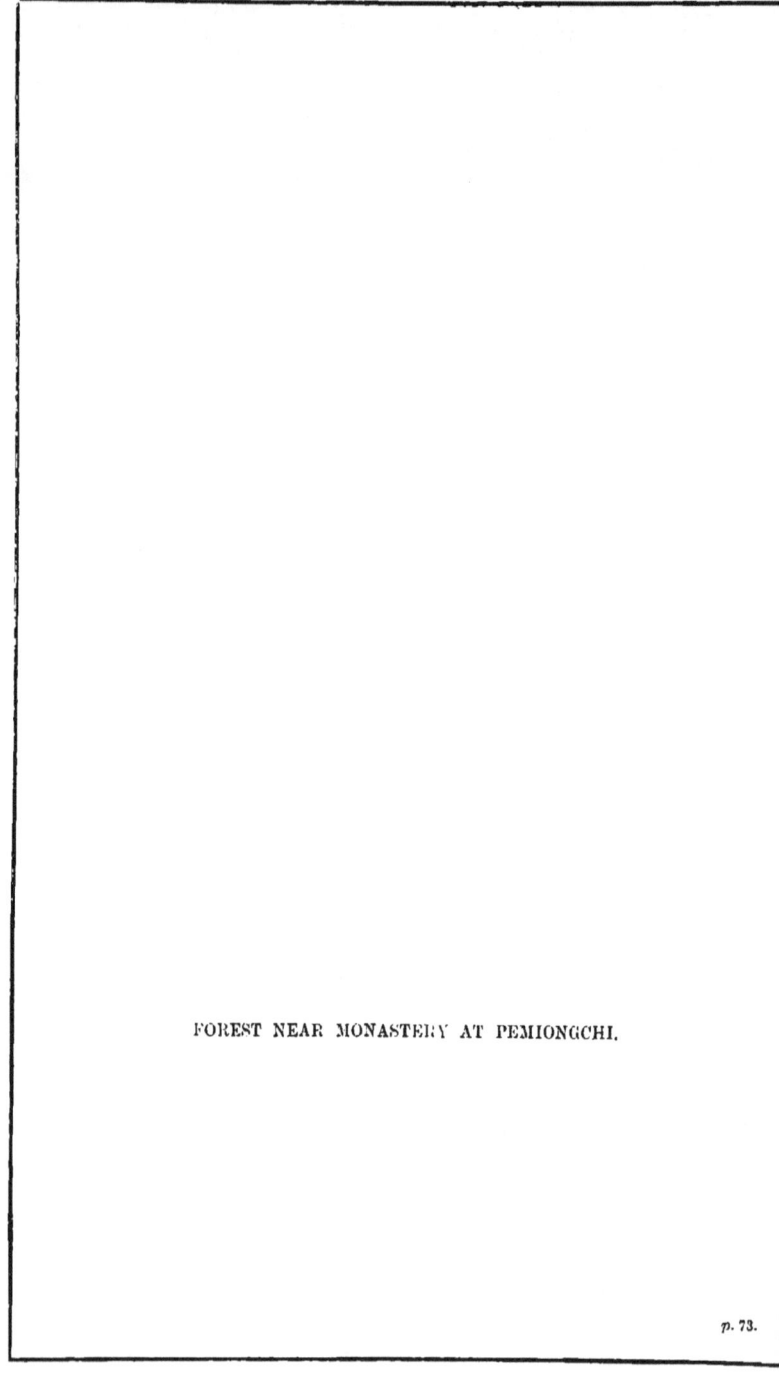

FOREST NEAR MONASTERY AT PEMIONGCHI.

Here a crowd of monks, in loose red robes and tall scarlet caps on their heads, received me with a flourish of cymbals and tambourines and most discordant blowing of conch-shells, thigh-bone trumpets, and Thibetan flutes; while a monk carrying a gigantic gilt umbrella, and others with long poles, from which hung richly-embroidered flags, conducted me to the head Lama, who was waiting at the door of the temple to offer me the usual silk scarf. After this all the monks went into the chapel. The head Lama took his seat in his official chair, the musicians put off the tall red caps, and, sitting down in their places, resumed the litanies for the dead sister of the Rajah, which had been interrupted by my arrival. I was taken to a seat which had been got ready for me opposite the lay-figure of the deceased nun, and was offered oranges, cakes, and murwa.

Our camp was pitched round a great chait, on a level spot about 200 feet below the monastery, in the midst of a superb forest of oak and other temperate trees; and here I spent four days, during most of which time I was laid up with a bad cold. I had much talk with the monks, and got much information from them. One in particular is a learned annalist, and we had many discussions as to the right dates of several of the leading events in Thibetan history. He disputed the accuracy of many of the dates given by the Desi Sangye, whose chronological tables Csoma de Koros obtained in Thibet. I have adopted the Desi's dates in this report; but I could not help admiring the ease with which my Pemiongchi friend manipulated the cumbrous system of the Thibetan cycles, and the rapidity with which he gave numerical equivalents for what seemed to me the hopeless puzzle of years, named after a combination of planetary elements and zodiacal animals.

Changachelling.

During my stay at Pemiongchi I visited the picturesque old monastery of Changachelling, which is really the parent, but which is now by far the least important of the two, owing, as the head Lama told me, to the disregard of the obligation of celibacy among the monks, most of whom were married. He said that the evil had now taken such deep root, that he doubted whether any reformer would be strong enough to eradicate it.

Pemiongchi to the Little Rungeet

The notes of my visit to the great monasteries of Tassiding, Pemiongchi, and Changachelling, contain a great quantity of matter of great interest, but which, as it seems to me, is quite without the scope of the present report. I shall therefore omit it, though with much regret, and notice briefly the remaining portion of my tour. On the 9th December I left Pemiongchi, and having stopped at Rinchinpoong that night, encamped on the following day at a place called Mintugong, near the curious flat of Dhurmden. This may be described as a great even ledge some square miles in extent, with hills rising abruptly from it on three sides, while there is a precipitous fall of many hundred feet on the fourth. The soil is exceedingly rich, and every inch of it is highly cultivated, chiefly with cardamoms, oil-seeds, and other valuable crops. It is mainly inhabited by Nepalese, who are numerous in this part of Sikhim, and also about Namchi. There are very few Nepalese in other parts of the country; and the Guntuck Kazi told me he would not allow a Nepalese to settle within his jurisdiction. When I asked the reason, he said that they wasted the forests; that they allow their cattle to trespass; that they made themselves unpleasant neighbours in other ways; lastly—and I believe this to be the true reason—that the people of Sikhim had suffered so much in past times from Nepal, that they distrusted and dreaded all Paharias.

Near Mintugong were some copper mines, worked by Nepalese, who told me that the Bhooteas have a great jealousy of the extension of mining operations. I found this to be the case. The people of Sikhim have a belief—perhaps connected with the Fengshui superstition of the Chinese—that attempts to make use of the treasure below the earth are visited on those living above the surface by sickness of men and cattle, and by failure of the crops. Consequently the search for metals is in every way discouraged, except in those parts of Sikhim which are under the influence of the representatives of Cheeboo Lama, or that of Lassoo Kazi, or of some others whose prejudices have been removed through intercourse with Darjeeling. I am therefore unable to make any kind of reliable estimate of the mineral resources of Sikhim. The Nepali methods of working mines, and of extracting the metal from the ore, are very rude. I should say that almost every mine is abandoned long before the vein of ore has been exhausted; and Mr. H. F. Blanford, who visited a mining village with me, told me that there appeared to him to be a considerable amount of metal still left in the refuse of the furnaces.

On the 10th I crossed the Little Rungeet, on my return to the Darjeeling district, though I did not reach the station for more than a week after.

In the foregoing pages my aim has been for the most part to put Government in possession, as far as might be, of materials for a decision on the various questions connected with Thibet, rather than to urge my own views

Measures likely to improve our relations with Thibet.

and conclusions; but perhaps it may be as well that I should now state my opinion on the points which seem to me of most importance.

1st. Negotiation with the Government of China.

In the first place, then, I think that Her Majesty's representative at the Court of Pekin should make an effort to get from the Imperial Foreign Office a declaration that the exclusion of British subjects from Thibet is not authorized by the Chinese Government, and a formal expression of the Emperor's disapproval of the interference of his representatives at Lassa. It is likely that this would be enough, and that it would be safer and quite as effectual as an order for our admittance, which might give offence to the anti-Chinese party in Thibet, and so put a weapon in the hands of those who oppose any departure from the policy of exclusion as full of danger to the existence of Thibet as a State independent of British India.

2nd. Visits of our officers to the Sikhim frontier.

In the next place, I think that our officers should lose no opportunity of cultivating friendly relations with the Thibetan frontier officers; but that they should not show an undue eagerness to obtain admittance into Thibet for Europeans—whether official or non-official,—as such eagerness would be very likely to strengthen the suspicion, felt by so many Thibetans, that our advances are really meant to cover a design of annexing part at least of their country. I should therefore say that the proper course at present would be to press the Thibetans to meet our officers as often as possible on the Sikhim side of the boundary, and not to make any formal demand that the latter should be allowed to cross into Thibet. Of course if the Thibetans asked them to go they might do so, but not otherwise. This would leave our officers more free to urge on the Thibetans the desirability of removing the present restrictions on trade than they would be if hampered with the question of their own admission into Thibet.

I have not been able to form a very decided opinion on the subject of the establishment of a frontier mart. On the whole, I think that the measure, if carried out successfully, might do something to develop trade; but this would entirely depend on the site chosen, and the way in which the mart was started. My first idea, which I still believe has many advantages, was to establish an annual, or perhaps a six-monthly, fair at Gnatong, or some other well-situated place in the uplands. With a good road our traders could get up to such a place from the plains in three or four days; and I believe that, at the beginning and end of the rains, the climate would not be found too severe for natives of the plains, while there would be plenty of firewood available. I think that many Cashmeree and Newar traders would live in a place of this kind during the rains of each year, and during the cold season go down to the plains to make their purchases and perhaps dispose of goods obtained from the Thibetans. At present, as mentioned before, these traders find it profitable to transmit to India, in payment of their investments, silver which has first to be drawn from India by another channel. This, of course, is owing to the cost and trouble of sending down bulky goods by the present circuitous and difficult routes. If there were a good road from the Chola range to the plains, in addition to other goods which now come in from Thibet, Cashmerees settled on the range would probably send down wool and Newars ghee from the surrounding pasturages. Such a mart at Gnatong, with the periodical fairs, would be in the highest degree convenient and attractive to the people of Thibet, who would thus escape the much dreaded

3rd. The establishment of a mart.

risk of getting fever and ague in the lower valleys. The Sikhim people, however, are very much averse to my project. They say that I much underrate the severity of the climate in this part of the range; that Gnatong and other places in the vicinity which I suggested as alternatives are situated far away from the cultivated and permanently inhabited parts of Sikhim; that consequently food would be very dear and difficult to be got; and that it would not be easy to protect property at such wild and distant places, which, from their nearness to Bhootan, would be exposed to raids of the lawless people of that country. Guntuck, the place which they recommended for a mart, has some things in its favour, as I have already stated, and a fair road could be made from it to either the Yakla or the Gnatuila; but it is not well situated as regards access from the plains. It is rather low and hot for the people of Thibet, who, besides, would have to pass through the zone of leeches and *pipsas* to get to it; and I doubt whether our traders would prefer the constant exactions and annoyances which they might expect from the petty Sikhim officials to the risk of even Bhootan raids. On the whole, I am not inclined to recommend that Guntuck should be chosen for the mart, and rather think that if it should not be found practicable to establish it somewhere on the Chola range, Dumsong might be preferable to any of the lower elevations of Sikhim. It is true that the distance from the Jeylep Pass to Dumsong is greater than that from the Gnatui to Guntuck, and that there are two low valleys to be crossed on the former route and only one on the latter. But to counterbalance this, the best route from the Thibet boundary to the foot of the Chola range is that by the Jeylep Pass. Then Dumsong is higher than Guntuck, and quite as well suited to be the site of a mart; while, above all, the authority of our officers could be exercised directly there to foster trade and protect traders.

But, after all, the question of a mart is of small importance when compared with that of making a road through Sikhim to the frontier. Although the construction of such a road would of course at the outset be regarded with much suspicion by the Thibetans, I have little doubt that if once it were made, friendly relations with Thibet and a trade singularly advantageous to both countries would follow almost of themselves; and without such a road I do not expect much good from other measures. It is a surprising thing that no steps should have been taken to make a road immediately after the Treaty of 1861; but I venture to hope that the matter may now receive the favorable consideration of Government.

<small>4th. The construction of roads and bridges.</small>

In deciding on the line which the road should take, two distinct and practically independent questions have to be considered: one is whether the section between the termination of the road from the plains and the point chosen for commencement of the ascent of the Chola range should keep the valleys of the Teesta and its tributaries, or whether it should follow one of the existing routes,—*i.e.*, that by Pheydong to Keu Laka, or one of those over Tendong to Guntuck or Kubbi. The other question is the choice of the Pass which should form the terminus of the road and the point at which the ascent of the range should begin. I have little doubt that eventually a cart-road, and perhaps a light railroad, will be made up the valley of the Teesta to the point at which it was crossed by Major Judge and myself, or even further; but I think that such a project would be premature at present, and that we should, in the first instance, adopt and

<small>Best line for road to take.</small>

improve to the utmost one of the existing routes, even though this would entail many needless ascents and descents which a line along the Teesta would avoid. We know something of the route over the hills, and could begin working on the chosen road without delay; while the Teesta route would require to be surveyed, and might then be found to oppose engineering difficulties of which we have no suspicion at present. Then, the road over the hills would be shorter and more direct—an advantage which, in the minds of hillmen, would do much more than counterbalance its inequalities. Again, though the Thibetan trader on his downward journey would have to cross fever-haunted valleys, still he could always arrange his stages so as to sleep on the hills until he got into the comparatively healthy plains beyond Sivoke. I have talked to scores of Thibetan traders on this subject, and have invariably found that they would prefer a road over the hills to one along the valleys. Many of them said that they would make shift with the existing tracks if the streams were bridged. I have no hesitation whatever in recommending that the ascent of the Chola range should be made from the foot of Lingtu; and possibly the route taken by Major Lindsay and myself would afford the best line for a road, though, as I have already said, I should make an attempt to avoid the ascents and descents of the Lingchung range by taking the road up the valleys of the Rilli and the Lingtam for a few miles.

Urgent need of bridges.

If my present recommendation should meet with the approval of Government, and if it should be found possible to avoid the lower crossing of the Rilli, two large bridges would be required—one over the Teesta, which Mr. Tyndale, the Executive Engineer of the district,

thinks could be put up for less than Rs. 20,000;
and one over the Rishi, which I do not think
would cost more than Rs. 6,000. The Rilli, if
it should have to be crossed below Lingchung,
could be bridged for about Rs. 5,000; and if it
were crossed higher up, the cost would probably
be still less. Some smaller streams would
require bridges, the total cost of which would
scarcely be more than Rs. 7,000 or 8,000. If
my calculations are right, the whole of the route
from this side of the Teesta to the Jeylep Pass
could be bridged for Rs. 40,000, or thereabouts.
It would be difficult to exaggerate the incon-
venience, loss, and injury to trade caused by
the want of these bridges. It often happens
that Thibetan traders coming down at the beginning or ending of the rains find one of these
rivers swollen by sudden floods, and have to
wait on the bank, unable to cross for days, with
their cattle and sheep dying around, while they
think themselves lucky if they escape without
an attack of fever. Many sheep and ponies
are drowned in the attempt to cross these
streams. I lost a pony this year belonging to
Cheeboo Lama's representative, Tendook, while
trying to get it across the Teesta, and I have
heard of other ponies lost in the same way.
The District Road Fund has put a ferry-boat at
the bridge over the Teesta this cold weather;
but it does not meet the requirements of the
traffic, and is very expensive. Last Christmas-
day I found at the river a party of Thibetan
traders, with forty ponies, besides sheep and
cattle. They had been already detained one
day on the bank of the river, and it took at
least another day before they were all across.
Now I am convinced that the existence of
unbridged and dangerous rivers like this on all
the routes to Thibet does much more to check
trade than any opposition it can meet with
from Chinese Ampahs or Thibetan obstructives;

and if we are unwilling to spend the few thousand rupees required for these all-important bridges, we can scarcely take credit for doing all that we may fairly be asked to do for the development of the trade with Thibet.

If the bridges were once built, it would be an easy matter to make the road. It would not be necessary to spend large sums of money on it at once, if a great immediate expenditure should not be thought desirable. Ten or twelve thousand rupees, well laid out at the outset, would make a fair bridle-path; and if the same sum were spent annually for some years in improvements, an excellent road would gradually get made. It would probably be well eventually to build rest-houses for native travellers at convenient places; but this is not a matter of urgent or immediate necessity.

Promises made by the Sikhim Durbar.

I shall conclude with a word of warning. The Sikhim Durbar have made many promises of assistance in the construction of the road, and I am convinced that they honestly mean what they say; but I doubt much whether they will be found able to carry out all the engagements which they are prepared to make. And it is certain that much tact, patience, and forbearance, will be required in dealing with them when we come to require the promised assistance. The supply of labour is the point on which they are most likely to break down, and our aim should be to work as much as possible through our own people, of course accepting gladly, and making use of, any help Sikhim should be able to offer.

GROUP TAKEN AT ENCH.

APPENDIX.

MEMORANDUM OF A FEW ROUTES IN SIKHIM.

By Major Judge, R.E.

10th November 1873.—Late in the afternoon of 10th November 1873, I started to join the camp of Mr. J. Ware Edgar, the Deputy Commissioner of Darjeeling, who was on special duty in Sikhim, and whom I expected to overtake somewhere near Toomlong. I decided to take the direct route *viâ* Namchi and Tendong, and camped the same evening at Badamtom, about four miles from the Rungeet Bridge.

11th November.—Proceeded to Namchi (5,608) by the road which crosses the Rungeet (818) by the old suspension bridge. After crossing the bridge the road takes a steep rise of about 1,200 feet to crest of spur above the Rungeet (818), and thence runs along the south face of the ridge leading to the crest of Tendong. This latter portion of the road has a very easy gradient. Camped at Namchi (5,608) at about 3 P.M.

12th November.—Proceeded to Timi (4,771) *viâ* Tendong (8,671). After leaving Namchi (5,608), the road takes a rather sudden rise to crest of Tendong along the ridge leading thereto; and thence, after following the Tendong ridge on an almost level line for three or four miles, it again dips towards the Teesta Valley, about 1,200, by way of Timi (4,771). The road from Tendong (8,671) to Timi (4,771) is steep, but the face of the hill down which it diverges is broad. Zigzags of any required gradient could be made here; those traced in the year 1861 by the force under the command of Colonel Gawler are still to some extent in use. Reached Timi at about 4 P.M.

13th November.—Timi (4,771) to Lingmo (4,155). The road from Timi to Lingmo descends rather steeply as far as Turco, whence it runs for a few miles at an easy gradient along the slopes of Tendong, and then dips down into the Teesta Valley. The road then runs up the bank of the Teesta Valley along flat land for about two miles, crossing first the Rimpay stream and then the Rungpo (1,375). After crossing the Rungpo (1,375) the road ascends, at first by an easy gradient, but soon more steeply, to Lingmo (4,155), crossing two small, but rather deep, ravines midway.

Coolies, lightly laden, took eight hours' hard marching to get to Lingmo from Timi.

14th November.—Lingmo (4,155) to Tingtee (about 5,000). The road from Lingmo to Tingtee descends steeply to the Teesta, which it crosses at a level of about 1,600 feet by a cane suspension bridge, and at once ascends steeply for about 2,000 feet; thence it runs along the slopes of the left bank to the Teesta by an easy gradient to Tingtee (about 5,000).

15th November.—Tingtee (5,000) to Toomlong (5,368). From Tingtee the road continues to run along the slopes on left bank of the Teesta Valley until it meets the Ryott Valley: the best road to Toomlong runs up the Ryott Valley below Kubbi. But, as I was pressed for time, I cut across the Ryott Valley by a steep path, which descended about 3,500 feet, and again abruptly ascended 3,500 towards Toomlong, on the right bank of the Ryott. Both those paths were very steep, and in places almost vertical—quite impracticable for ponies.

After the path rises to top of the precipitous slopes on the right bank of the Ryott Valley, it continues along easy gradients to Toomlong.

The march from Tingtee to Toomlong took about nine hours, half of which was over steep paths. A traveller following this route saves a day's march; but it is not one that would be used with advantage, unless a person was pressed for time.

15th November.—On arrival at Toomlong, I ascertained that Mr. Edgar was on the opposite bank of the Ryott River at Kubbi, on his way down from the Chola Pass. Having ascertained that he would not cross until we had met, I went over to Kubbi (5,000), crossing the Ryott Valley at a level of about 2,000 feet.

17th November.—Kubbi (5,000) to Gyara Gong (5,325). At Mr. Edgar's request I left his camp for a week's trip, to explore the road to Sharab, by way of Gunduk, where we were to meet again.

The road from Kubbi to Gyara Gong rises by easy gradients to a ridge above it (elevation 5,325 feet), where it crosses the direct road from Darjeeling to the Chola Pass, about half a mile above Kubbi. Thence the road drops by a steep descent for another half mile to the village of Tincup, below which it crosses the Rathee-choo stream at 3,825 feet.

The Rathee-choo is only 50 feet broad at point of crossing.

Beyond the Rathee-choo the road runs along the face of easy slopes, in some places almost level to Gyara Gong (5,325).

18*th November.*—Gyara Gong (5,325) to Rongyik (5,400). From Gyara Gong the road rises to a ridge 6,125 feet in elevation, and then descends to the Rungeechoo by easy gradients throughout. It crosses the Rungee-choo at 4,725 feet. This stream is only about 40 feet broad, and is fordable.

Hence to Guntuck, or Ench (5,675), the road passed through Bartook (5,175). The ascent to Bartook is rather steep; thence onwards to Guntuck it is easy, and in places level. After passing Guntuck, the road to the Yakla and Gnalur Passes descends to Rongyik (5,400), above the Roro-choo stream. This road runs along one flank of a large spur, which rises in one ridge from Guntuck to the crest of the range of hills which form the Yakla Pass. The above road takes a slight dip midway, but has a very easy gradient as far as Rongyik. Thence to the Roro-choo it is not so easy, but is everywhere practicable for ponies.

19*th November.*—Started at 8 A.M. from Rongyik; crossed Roro-choo (4,550) by a bridge at 9 A.M.: breadth of stream 95 feet.

The road from the Roro-choo ascends along the ridge of one spur to the crest of a hill overlooking the Rongnee and the Roro-choo. The total rise along this spur is from 4,550 to 10,750; in all 6,200.

Aneroid readings at the following intervals during the day's march give some idea of the steepness of the ascent:—

Guntuck-choo (9 A.M.)	4,550
After 20 minutes' halt to take photographs (10 A.M.)	5,675
Yaks' hut at Rongshi (11 A.M.)	7,025

After half hour's halt for breakfast

(12-40 P.M.)	8,100
(1-15 P.M.)	8,875
(1-30 P.M.)	9,200
Piloom (1-40 P.M.)	9,500
Halted 20 minutes at Piloom, to get water from a stream off the roadside, some distance (2-30 P.M.)	10,050
(3 P.M.)	10,425

It began to snow at 4 P.M., shortly after our arrival in camp. The road passed over this day was in all parts practicable for ponies, and is much used by Thibet pony-dealers; but in many places the gradient is difficult, and might be much improved by a few serpentine bends along the brow of the spur. The general alignment of the upper portion of the road could also be much improved by leaving the ridge of the spur, and taking the direction of a saddle to the north of it. This alteration would rather shorten the road to the Sharab Pass, and eliminate the worst portion of it.

20th November.—Started at 7-30 A.M. from camp (10,425 feet), and at 8-15 A.M. crested, at an elevation of 10,750 feet, the brow of hill at the top of spur that rises from the Ro-Ro. Thence the road runs along a nearly level ridge into a gorge, descending at one point (where it crosses a saddle) to 10,300 feet, and passing through fir forests. After leaving the saddle, the road makes a slight dip; but soon begins to ascend along the right bank of one of the tributaries of the Rongnee, to a height of 10,925, where it crosses a stream which is an affluent of the same, and which runs down the valley of the Yakla Pass.

At this point there is a bridge about 85 feet long. We crossed this bridge at 11-30 A.M., after an hour's halt for breakfast.

The ascent from this bridge to the Tanyek-so lake is gradual and easy, along the right bank of the stream which flows out of the lake and runs into the Rongnee river. We reached the lake at 2 P.M., and after a halt of half an hour for photography, proceeded about half a mile along the right bank of the lake, and thence to the saddle at the head of the valley in which the lake lies. After crossing this saddle, the road descends along the face of some small hills, and again rises rather abruptly in the gorge of a steep ravine. After ascending this ravine, it again dips by an easy gradient to Sharab, the height of which I make to be approximately 15,000 feet,—water boiling at this height at 184° when the temperature of the air was 10°.

21*st November.*—Started at 8 A.M. to see the Jeylep-la Pass, as I found that the barometer I had with me only took readings up to 11,000, and the boiling thermometers were not reliable. I contented myself with taking the following bearings from the Jeylep-la Pass with a prismatic compass:—

In Thibet.
- To Chumalari ... ... 35°
- ,, Kazi Goombah 30°
- ,, Killum-see ... ... 20°
- ,, High Peak Pemla, W. of Chumalari ... ... 50°
- ,, Jeylep-la Valley ... 210°
- ,, Jeylep-la Ridge ... 280°

I returned from the Jeylep-la Pass to Sharab the same afternoon at about 4 P.M.

22*nd November.*—Started with guide at 7 A.M. to the Yakla Pass, sending the coolies back to the bridge below the Tanyek-so Lake, which I had passed two days before.

I reached the Yakla Pass at 10 A.M., thence taking compass bearing as under:—

To Chumalari ... ... 43°
High Peak to W. of Chumalari ... 64°

From the Yakla Pass I returned a long portion of the route I had gone over in the morning, but after proceeding along it about two miles struck off across a ridge into the valley which leads direct up to the Yakla through Byntan. I did not overtake the coolies at the junction of the Sharab and Yakla Valleys till 3-30 P.M. This route to the Yakla Pass is only practicable for yaks and coolies, and the route is in every way a difficult one. The worst portion of the route can be avoided by going up the Sharab Valley to the Yakla Pass; but the Yakla Pass is in every respect one to be avoided.

After rejoining the coolies, I proceeded the same evening as far as possible down the spur overlooking the Ro-Ro, by which I had made the ascent to Sharab. We camped at 6 P.M. at an elevation 9,525, at the first place where water was procurable on the descending spur. It had snowed slightly the two days I was up at the Passes, and the coolies were glad to make a forced march to get down to a lower elevation, where firewood was plentiful and the cold less intense.

23rd November.—Piloom (9,525) to Guntuck (5,675). Proceeded to Guntuck by the same route I have travelled over a few days before, and rejoined Mr. Edgar's camp.

In my opinion, the road from Guntuck to Sharab is one that follows, on the whole, a good line, and could with very little difficulty be made into an excellent road suitable for all purposes except wheeled traffic.

24th and 25th November.—Halted at Guntuck, taking photographs and making inquiries into extent of the water-supply and available sites for camps and building. There are six good springs of water at Guntuck, and ample space for sites suitable for a fair; also for a village as large as any in Sikhim.

26th November.—Guntuck (5,675) to Rumtik (5,325). I did not take the direct road from Guntuck to Rumtik, as I wished to ascertain if Sharab Ridge could not be approached by way of the left bank of the Ro-Ro-choo. For this purpose I descended to the Ro-Ro-choo by a steep path leading from Guntuck, and crossed over to the Pabyo Monastery (5,575) on the opposite spur. This path crossed the Ro-Ro (which was fordable with difficulty) at a level of 3,575 feet.

A road passing through Pabyo would have no advantage over, or be so convenient as, that *viâ* Guntuck to Sharab.

From Pabyo Monastery (5,575), I descended by a very steep path and crossed the Ro-Ro and Rongnee, or Burtup-choo Rivers, to the foot of the Rumtik spur. There is much flat land in the valley at the junction of the above rivers, which meet at an elevation of about 2,800 feet.

The direct road from Dikkeeling to Guntuck and Toomlong crosses over the flats alluded to. The ascent of the path from the Burtup-choo (2,800) to Rumtik Monastery (5,325) is tolerably easy, and through much well-cultivated land.

27th November.—Rumtik (5,325) to Sang (4,800). This road commences with a steep ascent to the crest of ridge overlooking Rumtik spur, and to an elevation of 6,625; thence it dips yet more steeply to Mertam (4,625). The ground about Mertam forms a succession of easy slopes very highly cultivated, and the road runs for some distance along an easy gradient till it passes out of the Mertam Valley, over a ridge 5,775 feet, into next valley of Orong-choo, where it crosses the stream of that name at a level of 4,025 feet; thence the road again ascends to Sang, 4,800 feet.

28th November.—Sang (4,800) to Rungpo Tang, on the Teesta (1,375). After leaving Sang the road runs almost level for some distance, and then turns the spur and runs along the face of a range of hills fronting Tendong. It takes an easy descent to Kamdong (4,225). Beyond Kamdong the road descends steeply to the Teesta (1,575), where there is a good cane bridge and also a raft.

From the Teesta bridge the road runs up the right bank of the valley, and after about a mile cuts into the direct road from Darjeeling to Toomlong *vid* Tendong. The road from the Teesta bridge to our camp at Rungpo Tang was nearly level—in many places quite so, and ran along broad level flats about one-fourth of a mile wide.

29th November.—Rungpo Tang (1,375) to Yangong (5,225). Our route this day left the road to Toomlong, and steeply ascended a large spur from Meinam Hill, on which Yangong Monastery is situated. The first portion of the road was steep, as usual in all ascents from the deep valleys of Sikhim; but after passing the village of Gajoong (3,000) it became less so. The whole day's march was, however, a steep one, along roads below the average of those usually met with in Sikhim.

30th November.—Yangong (5,225) to Lingdam (5,349). After leaving Yangong the road rises for a short distance, and then again dips by a slight incline to 5,400 feet. After proceeding on a level for a short distance it passes the village of Pading, whence it takes a steep descent to the Ringpo river, crossing it at 4,225 feet.

The Ringpo crossing is about 80 feet wide, between steep gravelly banks of very loose formation. The stream runs down a steep incline at a rapid pace, and can never be very deep. After crossing the Ringpo, there is a steep rise to the ridge overlooking the great Rungeet Valley. This ridge is a spur of the Mainom Hill, and is 6,824 at the point where it crosses by the road. After passing through a very fine forest, which descends to 5,625, the road emerges again on clearings near

Lingdam. The march from Yangong to Lingdam took less than five hours of fairly easy walking.

1st December.—Halted at Lingdam.

[*N.B.*— From crest of pass from Teesta to Rungeet there are two paths,—one leading to Tendong, another in the opposite direction, to Ralong Monastery, and also to the top of Mainom Hill.]

2nd December.—Lingdam (5,349) to Tassiding (4,850). This road runs almost level as far as Chosing (5,100), whence there is a road leading direct to Pemiongchi, *viâ* the Gyaring Mendong spur of the Pemiongchi ridge beyond the great Rungeet.

We, however, descended by a steep path, which crosses the great Rungeet higher up-stream, and leads direct to Tassiding (4,850). This road crosses the Rungeet at 2,225 feet. The descent to it is very steep, and the ascent to Tassiding equally so; but is practicable for mules or good ponies.

3rd December.—Halted at Tassiding. During the day I paid a visit to the Monastery of Sunning, which is on the top of the spur overlooking Tassiding, and connected with it by a long narrow saddle, on which there are about a dozen fine chaits and mendongs (monumental tombs). The path to Sunning dips to 4,075, and then rises 2,000 to Sunning Monastery (6,075).

The walls of this monastery are decorated with views of Pekin or Lassa (of the former as far as I could ascertain), and in a manner different to those of any other we visited. The architraves and capitals of the pillars were all plain gilt and carved; but free from the coloured ornamentation which is common in most other monasteries.

4th December.—Tassiding (4,850) to Pemiongchi (6,840). This road descends steeply to the Ratong river, after leaving the saddle below Sunning. From this point it descends steeply from 4,075 to 2,450 at the Ratong crossing. The Ratong is a broad and rapid stream, deep at this point, and running between a perfect grove of overhanging trees.

The ascent from the Ratong river to Pemiongchi is steep. It passes through the village of Satyong (5,475,) and thence rises even more steeply than before to the monastery at Pemiongchi (6,840 feet). Almost the

whole length of the road from the river passes through
very fine forest.

5th December.—Halted at Pemiongchi.

6th December.—Halted at Pemiongchi; visited Changachelling Monastery (6,950), on same ridge, about two miles higher up the spur which leads to the Sampoong range.

Visited also Rabdenchi, the site of old palace of the Sikhim Rajah, and where there are also ruins of an old fort, the only one I have seen in Sikhim. It is situated near Pemiongchi, on the same spur and about 300 feet below the monastery.

7th December.—Pemiongchi (684) to Rinchingpong (5,866). Left Mr. Edgar's camp at Pemiongchi at about 3 P.M., and started for Rinchingpong on my way back to Darjeeling. The path I took descended the spur on which the Gyaring Mendong is situated, and thence descended very abruptly to the Kulhait river, which was fordable at this season of the year; but in the rains is a rapid and deep torrent, about 150 feet broad. The path to the Kulhait descends about 4,000 feet, and the ascent thence to Rinchingpong is about 3,000 feet, along a path in most places very steep.

8th, 9th, 10th December.—Returned to Darjeeling along the outlying spurs from the large ridge between the Kulhait and Rummam rivers.

The road crosses the following streams—viz., the Rishi, Torung, Rathoo, Rummam, and Little Rungeet. It crosses five spurs or ridges, making descents and ascents varying from 800 to 2,000 feet.

The Rishi and the Rothoo are both streams of some magnitude during the rains; and the Rummam and Little Rungeet are small rivers, only fordable during the driest season of the year.

No attempt is made in these notes to do more than briefly describe the leading features of the routes travelled over during a month's tour in Sikhim. The best of the routes follow mere bridle-paths. In the strict acceptation of the word, there are not any roads in Sikhim.

C. N. JUDGE, *Major*, R.E.

10*th December* 1873.

www.ingramcontent.com/pod-product-compliance
Lightning Source LLC
Chambersburg PA
CBHW020109170426
43199CB00009B/455